*Make Decisions Faster,*
*Make Them More Profitable, and*
*Make Them with Less Risk*

# *The*
# MONOPOLY
# METHOD

## An Insider's Guide to Navigating Wall Street and Becoming a Better Investor

## By Greg McCall

Rock Crest Capital LLC

ISBN-10: 0615493971
EAN-13: 9780615493978

gmccall@monopolymethod.com

# Table of Contents

# CHAPTER ONE

# The Monopoly Method
## A Better Way to Pick Stocks

We live in extraordinary times. Traditionally held beliefs toward the stock markets and the investment process have completely broken down.

Whether the risk is outright fraud by previously respected "professionals" such as Bernie Madoff; a collapsing financial system which took with it Bear Stearns, Lehman Brothers, and AIG; a global economic depression which resulted in millions of job losses; or unstable nations causing massive spikes in energy costs, the result is the same: extreme market volatility and risk.

Investing has never been tougher, and we can no longer blindly put our faith in others as we once did. It has never been more important to be in control of your own destiny. Investors, be they professional or not, need to become more involved with their investment portfolio.

Remarkably few people really have the right skill set to effectively manage a portion of their assets. In addition, few investment books truly lay out in detail exactly how to manage your investment portfolio—from investment research and selection to trading and risk management—in a concise, efficient, productive, and understandable format. This is what the Monopoly Method can do for you.

**The Seven Essential Skills and Insights of The Monopoly Method**

1.  Gain an understanding of the most valuable investment tools and strategies.

2.  Obtain an insider's view of how Wall Street works, the significant changes that have taken place over the past twenty years, and an investment road map for the next twenty years.
3.  Learn how to conduct your investment research in the most efficient and productive method possible.
4.  Receive an introduction to a proprietary and proven investment process utilized by a $175-million hedge fund to determine what to invest in, when to invest, and when to sell.
5.  Find out how to separate the investment signals from the noise.
6.  Understand how to manage your overall portfolio with the lowest risk.
7.  Find out how to incorporate market analysis and strategy into your investment selection process.

Everyone has heard the phrase: "He was in the right place at the right time." In one way or another, most of us are seeking this result each day, both personally and professionally. Occasionally, you come across someone about whom you hear it said far more often than the rest of us. Hockey great Wayne Gretzky was said to be able to anticipate where the puck *would be*, not just where it was, and that put him a step ahead of everyone else on the rink.

Being in the right place at the right time is what the Monopoly Method is all about. While simple and easy to understand, the Monopoly Method is also comprehensive and powerful. It will change the way you think and act while investing. It will put you in the right place at the right time. It will make investing fun, profitable, and less risky. And, most importantly, it will give you the confidence to take control of your destiny.

Who wouldn't have wanted to own Google at its IPO, Apple when the iPod was first released, or Sunpower, a phenomenally successful maker of solar panels, when it went public? The list goes on: early investors in Amazon made a bundle, and those who saw the changing fortunes of Monsanto did as well. The Monopoly Method would have identified each of these as a great opportunity. When you are in the right place at the right time, you will benefit by spending less time "looking" for investments and more time enjoying the fruits of your success.

**Being in the right place at the right time.**

The "right place" part of the equation is about finding and investing in companies that utterly dominate their markets—monopolies or near-monopolies. Few companies can be considered actual monopolies these days in the same way that Ma Bell used to have nearly *every* American as a telephone customer, but many companies still dominate a particular line of business, the dynamics of which offer the same powerful investment opportunity. A portfolio full of monopolies is going to make more money for an investor over time. A portfolio full of monopolies is going to have less risk. And a portfolio full of monopolies is going to be easier to manage. What could be better?

**A portfolio full of monopolies is going to make more money for an investor over a sustained period of time.**

Monopolies have an unfair advantage, and that is what leads to such great stock performance. They control their markets, making it difficult or impossible for others to enter. They have unique products that are not easily replicable. They—not the market—set the price of those products. They have higher margins, which makes them more profitable. They tend to be increasing their market share, thus growing revenues faster than their peers. Their management teams and employees are driven, paid very well to succeed, incredibly talented, and highly sought after. It is these characteristics that provide "abnormally" high levels of investment profits over time.

Consider the $44-billion purchase of the Burlington Northern railroad by legendary investor Warren Buffett in 2009. Why would anyone want to buy a railroad in the age of the iPad? Why would *Warren Buffett* want to buy a railroad, when he has enough money to buy nearly any company he sets his eyes on? Because it is a monopoly, that's why!

Burlington Northern, the nation's second-largest railroad, is the biggest (meaning highest market share) transporter of food and fuel products, such as corn, and coal for electricity.

Burlington Northern connects the U.S. to other countries. It ships a large amount of consumer goods imported from Asia through the large ports of Los Angeles and Seattle. The railroad also connects to Mexico, and is a prime beneficiary of the North American Free Trade Agreement (NAFTA).

While railroads may seem to be dinosaurs in an era of $250 coast-to-coast jet travel, they have far superior transportation costs to trucking. With oil and gas prices looking to stay high for the foreseeable future, Warren Buffet is clearly betting that Burlington Northern will take market share away from other forms of transportation. Some estimates peg that one train can take as many as 280 trucks of the road, saving significantly on fuel and environmental costs.

In brief, Burlington Northern is a company with market control, price control, high barriers to entry, a strong management team, and an ability to substantially grow its enterprise, both organically, through acquisitions, and through additional market share. It is a true monopoly with tremendous growth potential. This is what attracted Warren Buffet, and this is the type of company the Monopoly Method will help you find, invest in, and manage in your portfolio.

**A portfolio full of monopolies is going to have less risk.**

Monopolies have many advantages; chief among them is their lower risk to economic cycles. In fact, during economic downturns monopolies will often shine. They make strategic acquisitions or take advantage of weaker players by exerting market control. In stock market corrections, they are usually the last to go down and the first to come back! This is absolutely the place you want to be.

**A portfolio full of monopolies is going to be easier to manage.**

You may have heard a friend or investment advisor talk about "core" investment positions. These are companies that stay in your portfolio over long periods of time. The Monopoly Method will give you the tools necessary to find these core positions, to trade them opportunistically, and to manage those positions on an ongoing basis.

Of course, not all monopolies make great investments. For example, your local cable TV provider (Cablevision, Comcast, or Time Warner) or your local utility is a monopoly, yet most have not performed very well over time—certainly not well enough to fund your retirement. Finding the right company, with the right set of monopolistic tendencies, and—this is critical—with the right set of *growth opportunities* increases the probability of a successful investment. This is the "right time" part of the Monopoly Method.

Another key part of the "right time" is investment timing and feedback. Stocks are volatile, and timing your investment—both your purchase and eventual sale— is critical to long-term success. The "method" part of the Monopoly Method will provide successful and proven techniques for better investment selection, trading, and feedback to help you invest more profitably.

Imagine being able to look at a stock and within thirty to sixty minutes have a sense of whether it could be a buy, sell, or hold—whether it is even worth your time to research. This is the Monopoly Method *process* system at its core (chapter 6): eleven variables and a simple yet powerful scoring system (chapter 7) which give you the highest probability of investment success. As you will see in chapter 7, scoring each of these variables for Apple Inc. (in the fall of 2010, when I wrote this book) at a stock price of $250 leads to a buy rating with a score of 10.8.

The Monopoly Method will build *structure* into your investment process. Structure is what separates great investors from average ones. Structure will make you more efficient and productive.

The structure of the Monopoly Method has three parts.

1. **Philosophy:** Philosophy is the way one looks at the world. In this context, it is how we look at the world of possible investments. The Monopoly Method views companies with monopolistic tendencies and significant growth opportunities as the best long-term investments.

2. **Discipline:** The Monopoly Method uses a specific, scalable, and repeatable format to conduct research into possible investments.

3. **Process:** The Monopoly Method uses a proprietary process to take that research and use it to make investment decisions. That process is then measured and recalibrated for both success and failure.

Philosophy is imperative: you need to have a point of view, or your investment strategy is merely scattershot. You also need discipline. With discipline comes the ability to differentiate one form of due diligence from another and to distinguish relative importance. The due diligence system is the glue that holds the Monopoly Method together.

Process is the secret sauce for many investors. While there are thousands of investment funds in the world, each one does things a bit differently. The one characteristic they all share: mistakes. Everyone makes mistakes, but the best investors have a built-in process that helps them learn from their errors. By measuring our results, we become better investors, since with measurement comes adjustment.

The Monopoly Method provides a perfect strategy:

1.  A strong **philosophy** built upon identifying monopolies,
2.  A rigorous **discipline** to implement the strategy, and
3.  A consistent and defined **process** to select, manage, and measure investments.

One of the primary advantages of the Monopoly Method is the independence and objectivity it brings to investment analysis. We all get caught up in our beliefs about certain companies or investment styles, but many times we lack a system of checks and balances to make sure what we have researched actually translates into an attractive opportunity. Compared to prior generations, we are lucky to have an abundance of tools at our disposal to decrease the risks we take on when we invest.

This book starts with a primer on the investment valuation tools needed to utilize the Monopoly Method to its fullest extent, proceed to the framework, and then see how these tools are applied and where they break down. From there, it defines the Monopoly Method, provides examples of its use, and finally takes a look at market portfolio and market strategy, as well as risk management. By the time you finish this book, you will have all the tools, knowledge, and methods available to make informed investment selections. The Monopoly Method will be an invaluable resource that you will refer back to time and time again.

**CHAPTER TWO**

# Investment Methodologies
## The Right Set of Tools for the Investor

There are two primary types of analysis used on Wall Street: fundamental and techni-cal. While it may seem counterintuitive, each has been both extremely successful and completely disastrous, depending on what point in time one happened to employ it. How can that be? One reason comes from Economics 101: when one method of stock selection appears to work well, more and more investors will start using it until it doesn't work anymore. In Wall Street parlance, they say that the opportunity has been "arbitraged" away. Another reason: people are people, and sometimes we col-lectively change our minds. They don't call it the flavor of the month for no reason. In stocks, as in ice cream, tastes do change. To have the highest probability of success in all markets, then, a combination of strategies makes the most sense.

## Fundamental Analysis

To do fundamental analysis of a business means to analyze those things that are fundamental to its continued existence and success. That includes its fiscal health, its financial results, its management, its markets, its competitors and its competitive advantages. The key to successful fundamental analysis, however, is to see how all the above are *changing*. If they are changing for the better, it's an almost surefire bet that the stock will be on the rise. But if things are getting worse, look out below.

Financial statement analysis can be extremely complex or relatively simple. The most important characteristic is consistency. Taking a consistent approach to analysis will lead to better and (more importantly) measurable long-term results. As with many things in life, learning from our mistakes can be a very valuable tool when it comes to investing.

## Income Statement

While the income statements of different companies often look quite different, they all contain the same components: the revenues a business brings in minus the costs of running that business. Hopefully, the difference is a positive number, which means the business is profitable. If it's not, the operation is losing money, a condition that cannot persist indefinitely.

Within the framework of fundamental analysis, the goal is to compare a company's income statements over time—that is, to see if things are getting better or worse. There are two primary comparisons that investors pay attention to: year-over-year (this year's results compared to last year's) and sequential (this quarter compared to the previous one). The first gives a hint as to how the company's business is changing over a longer time horizon; the second as to how it is changing almost in real time.

There are four income statement items that are of primary importance. Starting from the top and heading down, they are: Revenues, Gross Margins, Operating Margins, and Earnings.

## Revenues

Revenues, or sales, are without a doubt the most important factor in the valuation and stock selection process. Simply put, investors will pay more for the stock of a company that has sales growth than they will for one that does not.

One of the most common traps investors fall into is to buy stock of one company that seems "cheap" compared to its peers on some basis such as price-to-sales. If one company is worth $400 million in the stock market and another just $200 million, for example, and both have an equal amount of revenues of $100 million annually, isn't the second one "cheap" relative to the first? It's possible, but the likely reason is that the revenue growth of the second is just half that of the first. In the stock market, as in life, things are usually "cheap" for a reason.

Before comparing one company to another, though, investors usually start by comparing a company to itself. Investors looking at revenue figures will want to know not just what the recent results have been, but how they compare to the past. Consider the following quarterly revenues for a company:

Q1 Year 1 = $100 million
Q2 Year 1 = $120 million
Q3 Year 1 = $150 million
Q4 Year 1 = $150 million
Q1 Year 2 = $150 million

It is likely that when reporting its latest results, this company will tout the fact that its Q1 revenues have grown 50 percent compared to last year's Q1. That's true, but what's also true upon closer inspection is that the company's sales growth has clearly stalled. Indeed, it's had *zero* sequential growth in each of the last two quarters and has been flat for almost a year!

Many companies have seasonality in their sales results, of course, where certain times of the year are always better than others. Consumer goods companies—think Apple or Best Buy—tend to shoot the lights out at Christmastime and then invariably have lower sales in the very next quarter. That's perfectly acceptable, and a strong management team knows how to manage its inventory and production to navigate those changes in customer demand. In such cases, the year-over-year comparison can actually be more important than a sequential one. If the holiday season is the only one that really counts for your company, the thinking goes, it's not as important to compare December sales to those from the back-to-school season four months earlier than it is to compare this December to *last* December. That's not to say sequential comparisons don't mean anything—they can often be cause for concern or optimism—but they may be less important for one company than another. Year-over-year comparisons also vary from one business to the next; in the tax business, software maker Intuit gets the majority of its revenues in the June quarter as opposed to over the holidays.

## Gross Margins

If revenue growth is the most important part of a company's financial story, gross margin is a close second. After all, if a company decides to sell something for $1.00 that costs $1.50 to make, it's going to see phenomenal revenue growth from consumers who are onto the bargain. But nobody can do that forever. If a business is not profitable, it cannot fund its own growth, and the gross margin is a measure of profitability—what's left over after you subtract costs from sales. It is often expressed as a percentage of sales, calculated as follows:

## (Sales – Cost of Goods Sold) / Sales

For example, if your sales were $100, and the cost of goods sold was $60, your gross margin would be $40, or 40 percent of sales. Similar to revenue growth changes, the trend in this percentage can mean the difference between a high stock market valuation and a low one. Continuing with the theoretical company, consider the following results:

| | | |
|---|---|---|
| Q1 Year 1 Rev =$100 | Gross Profit = $40 | Gross Margin =40% |
| Q2 Year 1 Rev = $120 | Gross Profit = $48 | Gross Margin =40% |
| Q3 Year 1 Rev = $150 | Gross Profit = $57 | Gross Margin =38% |
| Q4 Year 1 Rev = $150 | Gross Profit = $54 | Gross Margin =36% |
| Q1 Year 2 Rev = $150 | Gross Profit = $51 | Gross Margin =34% |

As you can see, in addition to sales flattening out, gross profits are under pressure (declining from $57 to $51), and thus gross margins are falling.

Focusing solely on year-over-year revenue growth in this case would lead to the mistaken conclusion that the most recent results are positive. With both sales and margins tending in the wrong direction, that is anything but true.

## Operating Margins

Like the gross margin, a company's operating margin is a measure of profitability. It is calculated as follows:

## (Sales – Cost of Goods Sold – Operating Expenses) / Sales

Why focus on both? Because a company's operating margin can, in some instances, tell a much different story than its gross margins. Changes in gross margins tell you about the more important costs of manufacturing, while changes in operating margins tell you about execution of the management team. Managers have more levers to pull than just the cost of production, including how a company is financed (e.g., debt versus equity), how much it spends on research and development, or how aggressively it pushes its people and its equipment, a decision that might boost profits in the short term but which is unsustainable when people burn out or machines break down.

Savvy management teams use *every* tool at their disposal to wring the most profit out of a company's business without sacrificing its future or trying to deceive investors into thinking that things are better than they really are. (The fall of Enron beginning in 2001 was a perfect illustration of a management team losing track of what they were really supposed to be doing in favor of just playing accounting tricks on their investors.) On occasion, a company will report results that seem better than expectations but investors decide to punish the stock in spite of the news. We will talk about this (expectations) later in the book, but oftentimes the reason for the poor stock performance has to do with "how" they got to their results.

Investors in some sectors will pay more attention to EBITDA margins—or Earnings Before Interest, Taxes, Depreciation, and Amortization—than they will to operating margins. That tends to be the case in asset-heavy sectors that use a lot of borrowing to finance their growth, and investors want to strip out the costs of that debt and the depreciation of those assets and just look at how the business itself is performing. This is usually the case in cable, media, and telecommunications businesses, and some of the more cyclical industries, such as trucking, railroads, and resources.

## Earnings

The goal of investing is to make money on one's investments. The most straightforward way to do that is to find and invest in companies that are making money themselves—and making more of it over time. It should come as no surprise, then, that Wall Street goes into a frenzy every three months during "earnings" season, when publicly traded companies file their financial statements with the Securities and Exchange Commission.

Earnings are so crucial to stock performance that the ratio of a stock price to a company's earnings per share—its price-to-earnings (P/E) ratio—is widely considered *the* benchmark for valuation. It is, in the simplest sense, the amount investors are willing to pay for each dollar of a company's earnings. The lower it is, the "cheaper" the stock.

At the same time, earnings per share cause the most confusion and stock volatility during the quarterly financial reporting season. Unlike revenues, which (usually) are what they are, earnings can be manipulated or "managed" through such maneuvers as share buybacks or aggressive accounting and tax management. For this reason, it is critical that earnings analysis be only one leg of income statement analysis, the others being revenue and margin analysis.

The use of P/E ratios in isolation can be misleading to an investor. Just because a stock might have a low P/E ratio, for instance, does not mean that in the future it will have a higher one. Because of the economics of some industries, including growth and profitability, investors are prepared to pay higher P/E ratios for some versus others. Financial services stocks, for example, have always traded at lower P/E ratios than those of software companies. Buying one of the former because it appears cheaper than one of the latter is an exercise in futility.

Even when you're considering stocks in the same industry, there is usually a simple explanation for why one may trade at a dramatically different P/E ratio than another. Beware the argument that says, "Buy XYZ instead of ABC, because XYZ is trading at a P/E ratio of 10x versus ABC's ratio of 20x." While it might just be a hot stock tip, it is more likely to be explained by the fact that ABC's earnings or revenues are growing twice as quickly, or because XYZ is so inefficient that it only makes $0.50 on every widget it sells compared to ABC's profits of $1.00 on the very same item.

More often than not, there is going to be less downside risk in buying one stock that is trading at 5x earnings versus another trading at 40x earnings, especially if the former is in what appears to be a temporary rough patch that makes its current price a "value." The one trading at 40x earnings is surely that of a fast-growing company that will get punished by investors if it doesn't keep up its torrid pace. Whether you like cheap stocks, commonly referred to as "value investing," or more expensive "momentum investing" growth stocks, which trade with a higher P/E, your focus should always be on the strength or weakness of the "growth components" of underlying revenues, margins, and earnings.

### The Keys to Stock-Picking Success for the Income Statement: Focus on Growth and Margins

You can hear and read an infinite number of things about stock picking from an infinite number of sources, but there are two crucial things you must remember.

First: look for growth, and look for it on the top line first. Does a company have it, and can it keep delivering it? Simply put, do you understand a company's product, its customers, and the size of its potential market? It is important to fully understand and believe in the market opportunity and the competitive positioning of any investment selection. When it comes to growth, it's all about making comparisons. How fast has the company been growing over the past year, as compared to its peers, its end markets, and its own history? A company may look as if it is in growth mode, but with concentrated analysis, you can spot fool's gold as often as not.

Second: look for profitability, in the form of solid margins. How do the company's margins compare to those of its peers? Are they higher or lower? What are the dynamics of its margin profile? What is the direction of margins? The greatest potential for a successful investment will come from a company with improving margins.

## Balance Sheet

While investors pay a disproportionate amount of attention to a company's income statements, an understanding of its balance sheet—which tells you what it owns (its assets) and what it owes (its liabilities)—is a crucial part of stock selection. Analysis of a few key data points, in fact, can add valuable depth to an understanding of a company's overall prospects. The four most important items to focus on are: Days Sales Outstanding (DSOs), Inventory Levels (DSI), Cash, and Debt.

## Days Sales Outstanding (DSOs)

A company's revenues are what you might call a first-order data point: simply put, how much did it sell? Days sales outstanding is a second-order data point, but nearly as important: how long does it take the company to collect payment for those sales? The first (revenues) tells you more about *quantity*. The second (DSOs) tells you something about *quality*. If no one feels the need to pay a company, it's probably not one you want to bet on.

Specifically, DSOs measure the average amount of days it takes for a company to collect revenue after a sale is made. The formula is as follows:

### (Accounts Receivable / Total Sales) * 365 days

Cash is important to running a business. And collecting on sales quickly is a sign of strength when dealing with customers. If a company has so much demand for its products that buyers are lining up to pay cash, its DSOs can come close to zero. (In some cases, such as with Dell Computer, DSOs are negative, meaning the company gets its money—you pay for your computer—before it delivers the product.) On the other hand, if a company needs to extend credit to its customers in order to convince them to buy, then DSOs will be on the rise. Keeping in mind that investors are obsessed with change, a company that has *declining* DSOs is likely to attract interest. Conversely, if DSOs are expanding, the business may be weakening, and investor interest may do the same.

## Inventory Levels (DSI)

Just as the ability to collect payment for sales is important, so too is the ability of executives to manage the company's inventory. A company can make as many widgets as it wants, but if all it is doing is storing them in warehouses in hopes that they might one day sell, things aren't likely to turn out wonderfully in the end. To get a read on this, smart investors, in addition to looking at the total amount of inventory and its actual changes from period to period, look at what's known as Days Sales of Inventory, or DSI.

Calculating days of inventory helps an investor understand how long it takes a company to turn its inventory into sales, and the quicker the sale, the better. The formula is as follows:

**(Inventory / Cost of Goods Sold) * 365**

If a company is building inventory—in which case its DSI is increasing—it runs the risk of product obsolescence as well as the certainty of storage costs. In addition, the longer the product sits on the shelves, the higher the odds that a company might have to write it off entirely, thereby taking a charge against earnings in the future. Investors naturally prefer those companies with a DSI that is stable or decreasing.

Savvy investors will look at DSI at various levels of the "supply chain" to give them an enhanced understanding of a company's prospects. Consider the technology industry. While some investors are obsessed with communications equipment maker Cisco's financial results because they own the stock, others are obsessed with it because they own the stock of companies that *supply* Cisco with some of its raw materials. Communications chip makers Broadcom and Marvell Technology are both heavily dependent on Cisco for sales. If Cisco's inventory levels (DSI) are rising, there's a good chance sales growth at Broadcom and Marvell might be in for a breather.

## Cash

Generally, cash-rich companies—those with zero debt and lots of cash (and cash equivalents such as short-term investments)—serve to comfort investors, especially during times of distress in the financial markets. However, cash can also be a very useful investment analysis tool, particularly when companies or stock markets face difficult times. Cash levels can help investors pick attractive entry points.

When looking at cash, it's important to keep a few things in mind. The first—and we know this from our own lives—is that a pile of cash isn't worth much if it's sitting next to an even bigger pile of debts. For that reason, it's important to look at a company's net cash, which is its cash level minus the amount of debt on its balance sheet.

## Net Cash Per Share = (Cash – Total Debt) / Shares

During difficult market environments or if a company is executing poorly, a stock will often sell off significantly, many times ignoring key balance sheet strength measures. The reason is simple: people want out. They don't want to hold the stock, creating more sellers than buyers without regard to price and valuation. In these cases, stocks can sell off to levels that approach or fall below the value of the net cash (cash minus total debt) on a company's balance sheet. This can be a very attractive entry point. After all, if the company closed its doors and let all the employees go, the cash would go to the shareholders. It's as good a downside cushion as you can ask for.

Finding companies with high cash levels as a percentage of their market capitalization is a value investor's dream. It gives an investor comfort and it gives the company time to fix its business. Of course, cash is no panacea. It can take time to fix a botched new product, loss of market share, or a failure to recognize a change in the end market. Many times companies never make it back. But it's a lot better than a company in a jam that has no cash at all.

It's important to consider a company's "cash burn rate." This is the rate at which the company is spending or generating cash each quarter. Is the company burning (spending) its cash pretty quickly, or is it building up a cash pile? If a company is using the cash on the balance sheet to run its business, then we really can't utilize this asset for valuation purposes.

Analysts will often give companies credit for a high level of balance sheet cash when it comes to setting price targets. After all, when you're buying a piece of a company, you're buying a piece of its cash pile as well. Consider Microsoft. Analysts expect the software maker to earn about $2.40 per share in 2011. Using a P/E multiple of 14x (approximate five-year average is about 15x), you might think that $33 is a conservative and appropriate price target for the stock. But Microsoft also has $37 billion of cash on its balance sheet—the equivalent of about $4.00 per share. Some analysts will add those two together—$33 plus $4—for a total price target of $37 for the stock from a current price of $25.

While the presence or lack of cash on a company's balance sheet is certainly of importance, comparing two companies' cash levels won't get you very far, except in the unlikely situation where you're comparing two companies that are nearly identical save for the fact that one is much more cash-rich than the other. In most cases, noting cash levels is more of an analytical starting point than an end, since there are many other factors that go into the investment selection decision.

## Debt

Debt, to many of us, is a dirty word. Because we hate to be in debt ourselves, we often make the mistake of thinking that a company with substantial debt is in an equally undesirable position. While that is sometimes the case, it isn't always. Debt can actually be an *enhancer* to a company's worth.

Why would we seek out a company in debt? The answer is leverage. The best companies can take the money they borrow and invest it wisely, generating a return to shareholders that exceeds the interest rate they have paid on that money. (Of course, too much of a good thing can be a bad thing: too much debt can mean a company is taking on excess risk.) Unlike with net cash levels, comparing companies' indebtedness is important. A company may be generating faster growth, but you need to be aware of the reasons behind it.

As with varying P/E ratios, investors in some sectors tolerate higher debt levels than in others. For example, companies in the wireless tower industry (those companies that own the big towers with the cell phone antennas on top) routinely have debt levels that exceed their equity by several times. This leverage results in very high cash flow growth. At the same time, it comes with low levels of risk. These companies have very stable revenues and earnings, which are fixed for years at a time. For example, a company such as American Tower (AMT) might have 90 percent of its revenues already booked a year in advance, so investors want leverage. Comparing leverage of one tower company to another provides you insights into cash flow growth.

Regardless of sector, though, investors need to make sure to understand how much debt a company has on the balance sheet relative to its overall value. Many investors pay attention to the debt-to-enterprise value calculation. The formula is as follows:

**(Short-Term Debt + Long-Term Debt)**
**/ (Market Capitalization + Net Total Debt)**

**Net Total Debt = (Short-Term Debt + Long-Term Debt) – Cash**

Investors also keep an eye on a company's interest coverage, a measure of its ability to pay interest on its outstanding debt. The higher this ratio, the better, as it indicates that a company is generating enough cash to pay interest while also keeping ample liquidity on hand. A ratio below 1 indicates that the company is not even generating enough cash to pay its interest.

The formula is as follows:

**Interest Coverage = EBITDA / Interest Expense**

**Free Cash Flow**

The power of "free cash flow" (FCF) as an analysis tool is often overlooked by many investors, mainly because it is not the easiest metric to analyze, calculate, or forecast. One might say that most investors (even professional ones) are too lazy to focus on it, given its complexity. However, the best investors will utilize this metric, even going so far as to make it one of their most important tools.

The power of this metric comes from the calculation of the "free cash flow yield" as calculated by the following formula:

**Free Cash Flow (FCF) / Market Capitalization**

This is similar to the interest rate on a bond, and in its simplest form, companies with high rates (and growing) are considered more attractive. Think of it this way: if a company has a market capitalization of $100 million, and has FCF of $10 million, its FCF yield is 10 percent ($10 million/$100 million). One could say that the company's stock should go up "at least" as much as the FCF each year, or 10 percent in this case, since it has $10 million more than the original $100 million in market capitalization. Put another way, if the stock didn't go up based on the increasing FCF, in ten years the company would have generated $100 million in cash, which would be equal to the whole market capitalization! When an FCF yield is coupled with a company that is growing its FCF, a very attractive stock opportunity is generally in the cards. Now, the opposite isn't always true; negative free cash flow or a low FCF yield might be due to a host of reasons, such as a large capital investment program, which may pay off big at a later date.

Free cash flow is derived from the following formula and is found on a company's cash flow statement. Variables needed for the calculation of free cash flow:

A. Net Income (NI)
B. Depreciation (Dep)
C. Change in working capital (WC) = Current Assets – Current Liabilities
D. Capital Expenditures (CAPX)

**Simple Version**
**NI + Dep – CAPX = FCF**

## Complete Version
## NI + Dep + change in WC (positive or negative) – CAPX = FCF

Most often, the simple version is enough, as the majority of companies try to keep working capital needs low. Also, changes in working capital are generally a very small portion of the overall equation. It's also important to grasp an understanding of the *sustainability* and *growth* of free cash flow, since it will relate directly to the performance of the stock.

## Other Fundamental Factors

There are other, less mathematical metrics that factor significantly in a stock's valuation and ultimate investment performance. A number of the more important ones are outlined below, and are the basis for a proprietary stock selection and management tool introduced later.

### Track Record, Volatility, and Expectations

Consider two different companies of similar size in the same industry. Over the course of a single year, both companies earn $1.00 per share in earnings. Does it matter how they achieved that result? Should the stocks of both companies trade around the same level regardless of the trajectory of their earnings? Or would one path create a more volatile stock?

| Company XYZ | Company ABC |
|---|---|
| Q1 = $0.15 | Q1 = $0.15 |
| Q2 = $0.25 | Q2 = $0.40 |
| Q3 = $0.20 | Q3 = $0.10 |
| Q4 = $0.40 | Q4 = $0.35 |
| -------------- | --------------- |
| Year = $1.00 | Year = $1.00 |

Company XYZ clearly took a smoother path to its $1.00 in earnings. Barring some other factor, its stock will trade at a premium to that of Company ABC. Investors prefer smooth sailing to choppy waters and are generally willing to pay a higher P/E multiple for consistency. Investors will have more difficulty discerning the true momentum of Company ABC's earnings and will "discount" its valuation.

However, in investing, as in life, there are caveats. The biggest one of all on Wall Street is that of *expectations*. The most volatile time for a stock—upward or downward—is when results differ from expectations in a meaningful way. If investors were forewarned and expected the exact results that Company ABC delivered, they will be unlikely to punish the stock. If Company XYZ, on the other hand, had led investors to believe that Q4 earnings would be $0.80 and not $0.40, its stock could be cut in half on the news. But if Company ABC and Company XYZ are actually two different futures of *the same company*, it is a near certainty that investors will be more pleased with the results of XYZ over those of ABC.

Track record, volatility, and expectations go hand in hand. A stock will perform far better if it matches or beats Wall Street's expectations on a consistent basis. Consider the case of Apple. For years that company missed analyst estimates, had poor growth, and delivered volatile earnings. The stock treaded water as a result. Things changed in 2004 with the introduction of the iPod. Earnings thereafter consistently beat or matched expectations, growth accelerated, and margins increased. As Apple's reputation has rebounded, its valuation has increased, making it a very attractive holding for most managers. Apple has become a stock that is always "expensive" relative to its peers, yet it continues to be one of the best-performing stocks in the market. The reason is consistency. Populate your portfolio with consistent financial performers and your probability of success increases dramatically. The Monopoly Method will give you the tools to do that. (Of course, Apple may well stumble again, and its stock would suffer accordingly. But using the Monopoly Method tools will help you spot the telltale signs of such a stumble before everyone else does.)

## Visibility

Consistency of earnings is what it sounds like: a company's ability to consistently deliver the results. Visibility is related, but with a subtle difference. A company has good earnings "visibility" if those results can be projected with a high degree of confidence beforehand. Take the example of cable television or wireless phone companies, both of which have monthly billable subscribers. Each has a high level of knowledge about its earnings three months out, much more than, say, a software or hardware firm that needs to find new customers to make each incremental sale.

Generally, the higher the visibility, the lower the sales growth and valuation you will receive. While this sounds counterintuitive, think about the cable company example above. Investors pay for growth, and most subscription businesses (cable, telecom, newspapers, etc.) don't have rapid growth. Perhaps, if they are lucky, they are growing their revenues at a rate slightly above the economy, thus the reason for a lower valuation. With low growth, these types of companies prefer to utilize dividends to supplement their stock prices.

In certain instances, which are extremely attractive, you get both visibility and growth—which ultimately means higher valuations and better, consistent, strong stock performance! This is the case in the example of American Tower presented earlier. That company has very high visibility, with as much as 90 percent of its revenues booked a year in advance. In addition to this, it benefits from three other important factors. First, it has strong pricing power, and is able to raise prices each year because its customers have no other place to go (i.e., a monopoly). It benefits from the high growth of the wireless industry, especially data-intensive smart phones. And it is leveraging up its balance sheet—more debt than equity.

Each sector, in addition to revenue visibility and earnings visibility, has other metrics that investors monitor closely for visibility. Investors in engineering and services companies such as Foster Wheeler and Fluor, for example, rely on order growth and backlog as indicators of future revenues. Monitoring their success in projecting this number accurately over time is critical to understanding the direction and valuation of each stock. Over time, Fluor has been awarded a consistently higher valuation than Foster Wheeler due to its better track record at such projections.

## Quality

When investors speak of the quality of a company, they are generally referring to its management team, its competitive position, and the overall consistency of the growth of the business.

The quality of the management team is particularity important when making investments. We live during extraordinary times, and investing alongside smart, diligent, proven, and honest management teams is crucial to the success of the Monopoly Method. A company's competitive position is usually a reflection of the quality of its product, its ability to price its product at a premium, and the efficiency of its operations. And consistency of growth is observed over many years of providing investors with reliable forecasts and strong growth in earnings.

Great companies have strong track records, among the highest margins in their peer group, and a management team that has stood the test of time. In the technology field, that means companies like Apple, Cisco Systems, and IBM. In biotechnology, that means Amgen. And in engineering, it means Fluor. Each industry has its own roster of standouts.

For example, during the difficult economic environment that ensued after the technology bubble exploded in the year 2000, Cisco Systems established itself as a great company by extending its market share, making strategic acquisitions, and restructuring internally. When the recession ended, its growth and productivity accelerated and the stock took off. In the fast-paced personal computer market, Apple has established itself as a high-quality company through strong innovation and leading-edge technology. In the energy field, FMC Technologies, Fluor, and Schlumberger have established low-cost, strong technology niches that have positioned them at the top of their peer groups.

## Building Your Own Financial Model

Building your own model—or at least understanding someone else's—can be a very powerful tool in your investment strategy. In the simplest sense, a model allows you to test various scenarios to understand the most crucial and sensitive parts of a company's business model. In building or studying a model, you also become intimately familiar with a company and its operations, thereby allowing you to assess potential success or failure in a quicker fashion. For example, it might not be obvious that a company beat its earnings projections through a lower tax rate—a so-called "low-quality beat"—if you do not have the model in front of you. The following is a link to a Web-based financial model that has been a standard at many investment banks for years. Whether you use it or build your own, be consistent: use the same format, and you will be amazed how much more quickly you begin to understand changes in a company's fortunes, for good or for bad. The model can be downloaded or viewed at www.monopolymethod.com.

## Fundamental Strategies

Once you are armed with the tools of fundamental analysis, it is time to employ them through the use of fundamental investing strategies. There are two main types of such strategies—growth investing and value investing—and also variations on each.

## Growth Investing

Growth or "momentum" investing is exactly what it sounds like: investors seek companies that are growing quickly in hopes that a doubling or tripling in a company's size results in a doubling or tripling of its stock price. Not surprisingly, investors tend to be willing to pay a higher multiple of sales or earnings for higher or accelerating sales or earnings growth. If investors see a company's growth accelerate from one reporting period to the next, they might extrapolate this achievement to the following year and bid up the stock to levels inconsistent with current expectations from Wall Street. Their bet is based on the belief that earnings estimates will need to be raised by Wall Street and the market might likewise adjust the valuation.

## Relative Growth

One of the more popular investment strategies is to select potential investments based on an analysis of "relative growth"—which is an investment that trades at a discount to its growth rate, be that revenues, earnings, or cash flow. You can use any of the three calculations, which are as follows:

**(Stock Price / Sales Per Share) / Sales Growth Rate**
**(Stock Price / Cash Flow Per Share) / Cash Flow Growth Rate**
**(Stock Price / Earnings Per Share) / Earnings Growth Rate**

The lower any of the above multiples are relative to their growth rates, the more attractive the stock is.

There is a secondary comparison to be made, which is also "relative" to some other level of valuation. Once you have arrived at a multiple of sales, cash flow, or earnings to its growth rate, you can then compare that multiple to its own historical levels (is it higher or lower?) or relative to its peers. Dramatic changes in either comparison are a sure sign that something is afoot.

Most investors are not familiar enough with a company to actually estimate future sales, cash flow, or earnings, but that does not obviate the need to be familiar with the growth rate of revenues or earnings to decide whether to own, sell, or even short a stock. The relative growth method helps to ballpark whether a stock is attractive or not.

## Value Investing

Value investors attempt to discern what a company's value should be, and invest in those companies which trade below this value, sometimes referred to as its "intrinsic" value. Profits are made as the market—which, in theory, prices a stock efficiently—realizes its mistake and adds value to the holding equal to its intrinsic value. While identifying mispriced stocks can be enormously profitable, one must remember that investors with the same information can come to two completely different conclusions over a company's intrinsic value. For this reason, a more popular method adds another element—the comparison to its peers. This is called "relative value."

## Relative Value

One of the most popular value-based strategies is to select a potential investment based on an analysis of "relative value"—which is a stock that trades at a discount to its peers, yet has the same long-term characteristics and opportunities. For example, a stock may be trading at a lower valuation—Price/Earnings (P/E) or Price/Sales (P/S)—than its competitors, despite enjoying similar long-term prospects. A relative value investor is looking for companies that have traditional value characteristics, such as high levels of cash, a low P/E, and a seeming lack of appreciation by the wider universe of investors.

Over time, assuming they maintain similar characteristics to their peers, most stocks will rise or fall to where these valuation metrics equal other companies in the sector.

## Technical Analysis

Technical analysis is a strategy that forecasts the direction of stocks or markets through the analysis of past pricing data. While there are those who dismiss it out of hand, comparing it to the reading of tea leaves, as a strategy it dates back to at least the eighteenth century. The Monopoly Method uses a combination of fundamental and technical analyses, leading to superior returns.

It's important to point out that technical analysis is meant to supplement fundamental analysis. It provides a secondary "tool" to understand or forecast the price action in a stock. Many investors rely solely on technical analysis as their investment strategy, but the success of the Monopoly Method is predicated on utilizing technical analysis as only one tool in the investing tool belt.

There are many different types of technical analysis, but as a basic tool, investors should be aware of and understand three: support and resistance levels, moving averages, and relative strength. These indicators can help you identify meaningful entry and exit prices for your investments.

### Support/Resistance

The easiest technical method for most investors to understand is the concept of identifying levels where stock prices meet resistance or support. While the basic idea is easy to understand, unfortunately very few people agree, when looking at a chart, as to where those points of support and resistance are. The following is a simplified example of how technical analysis allows you to dissect a stock's trading history for this purpose, and proposes how one might utilize the strategy:

## Figure 2.1 Cisco Support and Resistance Chart

CSCO (Cisco Systems, Inc.) Nasdaq GS
9-Aug-2010    Open 24.21 High 24.87 Low 24.20 Close 24.77 Volume 63.9M Chg +0.70 (+2.91%)
CSCO (Daily) 24.77
MA(0) 0.00
MA(0) 0.00
Volume 63,945,600

Has proved to be Strong Resistance.

Great Support!

Source: www.stockcharts.com

The chart includes two support/resistance lines that correspond to the price action of Cisco Systems, a monopolistic network equipment maker.

As of late August 2010, Cisco was trading very close to its resistance line at about $24.75. When the stock traded above $24.75 back in March 2010, it rocketed to over $27.00 very fast and that $24.75 price level then served as support. When it broke through the line, again notice how fast it moved to the next line of support at about $22.75. Think of using these support and resistance lines as levels that make you more bullish or bearish. If it is above the line, it enhances your confidence that the stock will continue to rise; if below, the odds favor weakness.

## Moving Average (MA)

Moving average graphs the average price of a security over a specific period of time. Generally, investors focus on the 50-day and 200-day moving averages to help smooth out or showcase a stock's short- and long-term trends. (Sometimes they focus on the 20-day moving average for very short periods.) The strategy that works most often is to buy or sell a stock as it approaches its moving average line, as it will provide either support (in the case of a declining stock) or resistance (in the case of a rising stock).

**Figure 2.2 Cisco Moving Average**

Source: www.stockcharts.com

Let's take a look at the Cisco chart in the months leading up to its present level. The moving average technical analysis provided many clues as to the stock's possible direction. Through the downturn of 2008, Cisco's price was technically weak, since it could not break above its moving averages on a consistent basis. However, in April 2009 things changed, as Cisco broke through the 50-day and 200-day moving averages and didn't look back. In this case, the 50-day and 200-day went from being resistance to support, and the astute trader would have used these levels as stop losses for an investment. Note also that the 50-day crossed over the 200-day in June 2009, generally considered a strong signal of further gains.

If we fast-forward to today, we see a weak technical picture of Cisco Systems. It is below both the 50-day and 200-day MA, and the 50-day has crossed over the 200-day in a downward-sloping pattern, the opposite of the positive picture it painted in June 2009. You will also note it has broken through the support levels from figure 2.1, suggesting the next stop is likely to be at the $21 level, or possibly at the $18 level. Not many traders or investors would be attracted to Cisco at this time.

## Relative Strength

### Figure 2.3 Cisco Relative Strength

Source: www.stockcharts.com

Relative strength is an indicator that measures the rate at which a stock is moving up or down—that is, its momentum. When a stock moves up or down rapidly, it could be considered "overbought" or "oversold," and the probability of making a profitable trade in the same direction decreases.

Developed in 1978 by J. Welles Wilder, the calculation generally looks at fourteen-day trading action. The calculation is relatively simple, yet it continues to be a widely used indicator among professionals:

$$RSI = 100 - (100 / (1 + RS))$$
$$\text{where RS = Average Gain / Average Loss}$$

Wilder normalized and simplified this calculation to turn it into an oscillator that fluctuates between zero and 100. This makes the calculation of extreme price movements easier to identify. In the extreme, a reading of zero, based on the typical fourteen-day calculation, would mean the price moved lower every single day.

There are many interpretations for the RSI, and all can be quite powerful depending on the market environment. Readings above the 70 to 80 range are considered overbought and readings below 30 are considered oversold. RSI can also be used to recognize divergence, such as when the stock price is moving up, but the indicator is moving down. In that case, one could make the conclusion that the stock has a high potential for correction since the momentum is in fact negative. As you can see from the chart above, toward the end of 2008, Cisco spent much time in the oversold region of the RSI, leading one to conclude that it was might be time to take a look at buying the stock, even if it was technically weak based on other metrics.

## Advantages of the Monopoly Method

Many of the fundamental and technical metrics discussed in this chapter are often used as the **primary** method of strategy at many investment firms. However, the investors who utilize the Monopoly Method have a great advantage—they are able to utilize and combine the best parts of each method. It is in this combination that the probability of investment success is enhanced tremendously.

## CHAPTER THREE

# Navigating Wall Street
## Separating the Signals from the Noise

Despite the fact that Wall Street itself is more under the gun than it has been in a generation, there is good news for investors. There has never been a better time to take control of your own investment destiny.

If at one time it seemed that the game was rigged against the little guy, that's because it was. Here's the way it used to work. The chief financial officers of publicly traded companies, people who would never talk to most individuals, talked all day long to Wall Street analysts or managers who held large positions in their stocks. The analysts and managers, in turn, would tell their firm's traders, customers, and friends what they heard before news or data made its way to the rest of us. Don't confuse this with insider trading, as most of the information is not secret, but often it can convey the strength or weakness a company is seeing in its business. And in the end, individual investors, being the last to know, profited little or in many cases lost significant amounts of money betting on news that other people already knew.

So what's the good news? Wall Street's impact on the stock market has never been more marginalized than it is today. An evolutionary process of marginalization, which started in the 1990s, has gained steam as the recent financial crisis hit its peak and is likely to be the norm going forward. There are three primary reasons for this marginalization.

First and foremost is the globalization of the securities markets. Over the past decade, investor breadth has widened substantially, such that the impact of any one "axe" (Wall Street parlance for an influential firm or analyst) on a particular stock has been greatly diminished.

Second, Wall Street compensation packages have been cut considerably as commission revenues have declined significantly. Trading used to cost about $0.05 a share; today it's less than a penny. As a result, Wall Street can't afford the same kind of infrastructure it used to use to keep its edge on the rest of us intact. The most talented analysts have left the "sell side" (Wall Street firms) and shifted to the "buy side" (investment funds) or have focused on investment banking revenues. This has led to lower-quality research and limited impact on stocks from that research.

Third, as a result of a more stringent regulatory environment, it's easier than ever before for small investors to get the same access to management that Wall Street analysts have. Most investor meetings, for example, are streamed over the Web, meaning that all you need to gain access is a computer and an Internet account. One morning in 2007, I got up early, rushed to the train, took it into the New York, trekked across town to a meeting, sat through the presentation, spoke to the management team directly, and then called my trader with the "unique insight" I had gained and wanted to trade on. His response: "We already have it." The information had already been e-mailed to him from someone who'd watched the presentation on the Web. In the Internet era, information travels almost instantaneously, and you are sometimes better off in front of your computer than at the meeting itself.

Now that we have a level playing field that all investors can play on, we need to tackle the issue of information relevancy. Meaning, how do we know which data is important? In other words, how do we separate the signals from the noise? There is so much information out there that investors can easily drown in the flood. And we're not just talking about making the initial decision to buy or sell a stock. We're also talking about the daily or weekly task of staying on top of your investments, meaning having an understanding of which information (signals) is critical to investment performance. Signals on Wall Street generally consist of data that affects—positively or negatively—the "expectations" inherent in a stock. Since all stocks discount a future prediction of financial performance, any data that potentially impacts this future is important.

Companies are graded—their stock will move up, down, or remain the same—four times a year when they report their earnings, and it's important to recognize any signals which may give you advance notice of their performance. The Monopoly Method will prepare you for earnings by giving you a sense of what is "priced in" to the stock, whether it is priced for high expectations or low.

Signals generally fall under three headings:

1. Earnings expectations, both published and non-published.
2. Positive or negative commentary from management.
3. Positive or negative commentary from an analyst.

Earnings expectations refer to the financial estimates—of revenues and earnings—investors are expecting when a company reports its financials. And while it is tempting to look at the estimates provided by Wall Street analysts as the "right" number, these estimates often do not reflect current knowledge and expectations. Investors are a smart bunch (most of the time), and are always seeking the "latest" information and trying to adjust the price of the stock to meet this information. For example, many times a stock will move up right before a financial report, only to have the company beat estimates and then trade down afterward. Generally, this means investors were assuming better financials than were reported. In Wall Street parlance, we say they missed the "whisper numbers." The Monopoly Method takes into consideration the current expectations around a company's financials and puts these into perspective.

When a company reports its earnings, generally it will set expectations for the following period or year. During the intervening period before the next reporting date company officials will often speak with investors or analysts at company- or Wall Street-sponsored events. It's important to know when these engagements occur, even if you do not have access, as the stock price movements prior to, the day of, and afterward can give important indications of the discussion relative to previous expectations. (Because of recent changes in securities law, you will always be able to get your hands on the transcript of a speech made by a senior company executive at such an event. It behooves you to do so.)

Lastly, analysts who follow the company perform industry research and speak to customers and competitors on a regular basis. If they determine that information they've gleaned differs from the expectations set for the company, then they might publish a new report. Since analysts generally have a current published rating on each company they follow—buy, sell, or hold—new information can either support or invalidate their current thinking. Keeping on top of analyst commentary is another way for an investor to get an idea of whether a company is on track to meet, beat, or miss expectations.

Unfortunately, there is one aspect of expectations that is very difficult to prepare for. When a company reports its earnings, as we mentioned, it will often provide information about the next reporting period. Working through a quarter to get a sense of recent performance is hard enough, but investors are in no position to guess what the management will provide as future guidance. The good news about this is that neither professionals nor individuals have an advantage. The best we can do is prepare accordingly and position ourselves in the companies that meet the criteria of the Monopoly Method. This assures us that over the long term, even if near-term guidance is unsuitable to our investment position, our chances for long-term investment gains remain strong.

### How to Monitor Expectations

As an analyst and manager for over twenty years, following the brokerage community has been an integral part of my daily work. Whether it's coming from management or the analysts themselves, they provide the running commentary around expectations. In essence, they help one sift through the noise to get the signal. However, given the marginalization of the brokerage houses, investors can bypass the brokers and achieve much of the same results.

### Real-Time Information Distribution – 2 Hours to 20 minutes

Early on, I developed and utilized an early morning routine, which would take roughly two hours. The idea was to collect data from each broker I worked with, aggregate the important data, and utilize it to develop my short- or long-term strategy.

There are six variables that are important and which generally have expectations (i.e., stocks will move based on the information) associated with them:

1. Overnight direction of international markets, primarily Europe and Asia.
2. Company-specific financial results, which can influence the trend of the overall markets or your portfolio.
3. Upgrades or downgrades by Wall Street.
4. Economic releases.
5. Specific events such as analyst meetings or industry trade shows.
6. Media reports, either in print, video, or on the Web, about positions in the portfolio.

The power of the Internet has brought these opportunities to individuals. Inexpensive services such as www.briefing.com are available that get you ***about 80 percent of the way there in 20 percent of the time***. Whether you are trading full time or have a different profession, take a few minutes each morning to review the data and focus on these six areas.

As an individual, it is likely you will have limited access to brokerage reports, which sometimes have strong reasons for upgrading or downgrading a stock. Briefing.com does a great job of synthesizing much of this information for you. In addition, many blogs and sites provide further detailed information. Some of my favorites include www.seekingalpha.com, www.marketwatch.com, www.thestreet.com, and www.wikinvest.com.

Of course, understanding the information in context is also important. For example, there have been countless instances where an influential brokerage firm will downgrade and reduce earnings for a stock. When the market opens the next day, the stock declines, but within a few hours the stock is unchanged or even up. Often, the reason is that the analyst responsible for the report felt pressure to lower his or her numbers to match those of other analysts. So, in effect, the news was already priced into the stock, as most of the other analysts following the stock already had their earnings estimates at this lower level.

The ability to understand and think about expectations is clearly important. Early in my career, within the first few months out of college, a lead story in the *Wall Street Journal* appeared to discredit and put a very negative spin on a health-care holding in our portfolio for which I was responsible. I remember walking into the office to cold stares from everyone, not an experience I would wish on my worst enemy. (I was a twenty-two-year-old rookie!) However, as I read the article, I realized the information had already been disclosed several months earlier. While still a baby in the field, fortunately my colleagues took my insight, and by the end of the day the stock was back up. This proved to be not only a valuable lesson for me, but gave me my first exposure to the Yale Club, with dinner courtesy of the president of my firm.

Briefing.com and other services, such as StreetAccount, also offer the ability to filter content. I would suggest at least four filters to start.

1. Earnings
2. Personal Portfolio Holdings
3. Followed Companies (companies you know or like)
4. Events

Firstly, a filter for earnings will show you what companies are reporting even if you do not own them. For example, if a steel or electronics firm is reporting a successful quarter, it gives insight into the particular market that these products go into—automobiles or computers, for instance—as well as the overall global economy.

Secondly, a filter can be used for the companies that are in your portfolio. For obvious reasons, you want to be alerted to information about your holdings.

Thirdly, a filter for all the companies you follow, which should go beyond those in your portfolio and include those possibly doing business with them, as well as companies you are scanning for potential investment.

One of the most common mistakes seen with analysts I have worked with is that, after working several hours to understand a company and eventually putting money into the stock, when they close the position, they move on to the next stock and forget about the one they just sold. This is a horrible mistake; you've already spent time learning about the investment merits of the company, so pushing it aside and forgetting about it is unproductive. By keeping it on a watch list and monitoring it, perhaps at a future date a piece of new information will attract your interest again and lead to a profitable investment. A good analyst may have only thirty stocks active in his or her portfolio, but can follow one hundred to two hundred companies and spot profitable opportunities as they come along. With the methods discussed in this book and a minimal time commitment, individuals should be able to follow at least fifty companies if they use the Monopoly Method.

Economic data can be hit or miss, but I find focusing on three metrics will get you most of the way there:

1. Industrial production,
2. Leading indicators, and
3. Inflation metrics, such as PPI and CPI.

Because China is such an important driver of global growth these days, keeping up with these same statistics for China will also help your overall perspective.

I have specifically omitted employment information as a fourth metric. While it is important and a measure of the health of the economy, history has shown it to be a lagging indicator, meaning that by the time it gets better or when it starts to get worse, the markets already know. For example, by the time we start creating jobs after the 2009 recession, the market will have already moved up significantly.

The last variable, and one of the most important parts of your ongoing due diligence process, is: *events*. Know what's ahead of you, so that you can be prepared! An event is an earnings announcement, a speaking engagement at a conference, an appearance at a trade show, or similar occurrences. Be prepared, as someone will be listening to the event to see if the information conveyed is on par with Wall Street's expectations.

### Access to Management

The sell side plays an important role as a relationship builder. Its members provide a conduit for meeting the management teams of the companies in which we invest our capital, although it is almost exclusively for institutions. There are two developments, however, that have occurred over the years which have leveled the playing field: the Internet and the regulatory environment.

When I first started on the buy side in 1990, one of the most important ways I differentiated myself was by understanding the power of gaining insight into a company's business by attending industry events and trade shows. These events gave me the opportunity to speak with salespeople and engineers, the lifeblood of companies. Most analysts did not attend these conferences, thus giving me a critical edge in my due diligence. Today, because of the ubiquity of the Internet, but more importantly due to significantly greater regulation, almost every conversation, meeting, trade show, and earnings report is available to the public through webcasts or conference calls, thus creating very little "edge" for institutional investors with fat wallets. *While individual investors may not actually meet management, critical information from management is now available to almost everyone who wants it.* If you enjoy the opportunity to speak with the management of a current or prospective investment position, however, I have included guidelines to such a discussion in the second advanced knowledge section.

Stocks move based on expectations, and knowledge of those shifting expectations is what separates strong investors from weak ones. Each quarter a company reports its financial performance, and investors have a chance to rate their success. Each quarter, when reviewing a company, I give it a simple grade, measured in a similar fashion to something we all understand—street light signals. A red light means it did not meet expectations and I should review the reasons I own or am considering owning the stock. Yellow means there were some minor negative issues that need monitoring (for example, its gross margins may have been a bit weak) for a movement to red or back to green. And green means the company performed according to or better than expectations. By focusing your research on those "signals" which relate directly to "expectations," the time you spend working on building wealth will be productive, profitable, and enjoyable.

Now let's take it a step further. On Wall Street, we know that information is everything. If you do not have the right information, and use it in the right way, then you are left with useless information and, most likely, wasted time. This section will help you separate the signals from the noise within each sector, since different stocks and different industries have different signals. It will answer three critical questions:

1. What is the important information needed to make an investment decision based on the type of company?
2. Where do I find this information?
3. How do I use the data I have acquired?

## Industry Analysis

Any conversation about investment analysis will touch on a number of common metrics: P/E comparisons, growth rates, or balance sheet strength. But it is *critical* to realize there is always a big difference between the information needed to make a decision in one sector versus another sector.

The way an investor conducts due diligence for a retail store, such as Wal-Mart, differs quite substantially than the way one might research a bank or technology company. Because diversification is critical to reducing risk, an investor needs to understand the key metrics to focus on when investing in different sectors.

## Industry Sectors

**Financials** – Includes banks, insurance companies, mortgage companies, credit card companies, and other financial firms.

**Industrials** – Includes much of the manufacturing base and transportation sector. Industrials are often referred to as cyclicals because of their close ties to the economic cycle.

**Technology** – Includes companies in the hardware, software, semiconductor, services, and Internet areas.

**Consumer** – Includes consumer-facing retail companies as well as food, lodging, and leisure firms. Includes businesses that are cyclical (move up or down with the economy) and those that are non-cyclical (stable or basic needs, such as food and health care).

**Energy** – Includes traditional oil, gas, coal, and nuclear service and equipment companies, as well as alternative energy companies in the wind, solar, and biofuel areas.

**Basic and Commodities** – Includes basic materials needed in the construction of other products, such as chemicals, paper, iron, and copper. Also includes commodities such as gold, silver, and fertilizer.

## Financials

It's a sure bet that most people never thought Bear Stearns and Lehman Brothers might collapse within six months of each other, or that AIG, an insurance company, could almost bring the entire financial system to its knees. But we live in extraordinary times. Many companies underestimated the risk they were taking in the marketplace, and that had catastrophic results. More than ever before, investors need a strong analysis skill set in order to invest in the financial sector.

One of the best-known financial analysts, Meredith Whitney, made her reputation by being on the forefront of this financial crisis as far back as 2007. How did she see what so many others failed to notice? Many of her views came from a due diligence strategy that we can learn from.

Banks, credit card companies, and insurance companies are in the leverage business. By loaning money at rates higher than they pay to borrow it, they lock in a spread. When the economy seemed strong, they inflated their balance sheets by adding on more and more leverage—i.e., they borrowed much more in order to lend much more—and lent it out to riskier and riskier borrowers.

That's all well and good, until your borrowers can't seem to find the scratch to pay their bills. When banks leverage their assets, they assume a certain percentage of bad loans (defaults), and in order to cover those losses and maintain regulatory requirements, they maintain a certain level of assets (cash).

But their models didn't foresee the magnitude and severity of the housing bust. When default rates spiked higher than their projections, many financial institutions were caught in a classic liquidity squeeze: because they were unable to collect from their borrowers, they defaulted on their own debts, and collapsed.

When analyzing financial firms, most of the general investment approaches—looking at revenues, margins, and expenses—are not applicable and need to be replaced by tools which measure a bank's loan and customer health. It is also important to monitor a financial company's customer and geographical exposure—for example, whether a bank is more exposed to commercial or residential real estate, consumer credit cards, or other sectors where problems have emerged. While there are many different types of financials, we will review four, and the top three metrics for each type that investors need to focus on.

1. **Banks/Credit Card Companies –** It is important to understand that most investors focus mainly on book value as a measure of value. However, book value can be overinflated and can completely misrepresent your potential downside. Banks' book values are derived from a measure of their assets. In order to agree that the book value makes sense, three underlying metrics should be looked at.

**Asset Quality:** It is generally difficult to assess the quality of a bank's portfolio, but we can get a basic idea of the quality by looking at the absolute level and the trend of non-performing loans (NPLs), often referred to as the loan loss provision (LLP) ratio. This ratio will also help you create a "normalized earnings" figure, by reviewing historical figures and adjusting it for the present.

**Yield:** While every investor likes higher dividends, this must be taken in context with the quality of assets, capital strength, and asset concentration.

**Capital Strength:** At banks, capital strength is measured by what is known as the Tier 1 capital ratio—the higher the better. It is also important to monitor lower-quality Tier 2 and Tier 3 loans, to perhaps gain insight into the future direction of the Tier 1 assets.

2. **Insurance Companies –** Insurance companies are in the risk analysis game. Similar to banks, they hold a capital position and underwrite risk against it. Generally, during stable markets, insurance companies should be viewed as having greater safety among financials due to better balance sheets, and thus book value is an applicable valuation metric. Primarily, research in this sector should include:

**Deferred Acquisition Costs (DAC):** One of the largest intangible asset costs for an insurance company is the cost of acquiring new customers. These costs are not expensed when they occur, but capitalized over time (a percentage is recognized each quarter). Thus, if an insurer is not adding to its base of clients, expenses could increase significantly. Usually this metric is expressed as an absolute dollar figure and is generally part of the firm's total intangible value assets.

**Asset Leverage:** This is the level of investments relative to shareholders equity. One of the main causes of the financial crisis that started in 2008 was leverage, which in some cases exceeded a 30-to-1 ratio ($30 of borrowing per $1 of assets).

Generally, a ratio under 10x is considered acceptable. Many in the insurance sector are under 8x.

**Investment Quality:** It's important to keep track of the percentage of the investment portfolio that is invested in non-investment grade securities or illiquid assets (such as real estate). While the rating agencies Moody's and Standard & Poor's have come under fire for their role in the financial crisis, they remain the primary source of ratings information about publicly traded debt instruments.

3. **Real Estate Investment Trusts (REITs)** – One of the best economic indicators for the real estate and construction sector is the Architectural Billing Index (ABI), which measures construction activity nine to twelve months into the future. The index can be found at www.aia.org.

**Net Asset Value (NAV), FFO Multiple (FFO):** Premium or discounts to the NAV is a useful measure to get a better understanding of where we are in the cycle. When REITs are trading at a premium to NAV, investors are pricing in a strong economic outlook. While P/E is a useful measure for this sector, many REITs report Funds From Operations (FFO) as well, and Price-to-FFO can be an important gauge also.

**Geography/Property Type:** Every REIT or property stock has different exposure to different types of real estate, from malls to office space, commercial versus residential, international versus domestic, and regional versus national. It is important to gain a view into where any particular cycle is at that moment in time. For example, in October 2009 residential real estate looked to be bottoming, but commercial real estate showed continued downside risk.

**Leverage:** Similar to other financials, leverage can enhance returns as well as extend risk. Generally, leverage risk in REITs is characterized by interest coverage ratios, such as Debt/EBITDA. Ratios of 4x to 6x are generally considered acceptable. Ratios higher than 6x are considered excessive.

4. **Brokerage Firms/Investment Banks** – Despite changing regulations, higher capital requirements, and uncertain economic and headline concerns, the best brokerage firms have the ability to generate superior earnings and book value growth both in the near and long term. Their size allows them to capitalize on and create liquidity in the markets they address. Factors to review include:

**Market Share:** Market share in this sector is critical, considering the large percentage of earnings that come from the investment banking and trading business.

Given the risk of today's economy, companies such as Goldman Sachs and Morgan Stanley have tremendous scale advantages.

**Tangible Book Value:** Traditional valuation measures of book value fall short for financial companies, so a better valuation measure is tangible book value. This is defined as the book value minus intangible assets (such as goodwill) that would not be recognized in the event of a bankruptcy-induced liquidation. The tangible book value per share (TBVPS) formula utilized to value a company is the tangible book value divided by common shares outstanding.

**Leverage:** During the crisis that led to the liquidation of both Bear Stearns and Lehman Brothers, leverage went from being a key growth attribute to the death knell for those that used it in excess. Levels of leverage for the group have come down from the mid-thirties (meaning they borrowed $30 for every $1 they had) to the mid-teens. While this seems high, it is very reasonable if risk is managed appropriately. Understanding where a brokerage firm's leverage ratio lies will provide a perspective on the quality of its growth.

**Risk Weighted Assets (RWA)/Total Assets (TA):** Another important measure which serves to help investors understand the potential growth for a brokerage firm is the RWA divided by total assets. Similar to leverage, this metric in effect gives an investor an understanding of how much money is "at work." Too low—below 40 percent—and a brokerage firm is not utilizing its balance sheet effectively. If the ratio is too high—over 70 percent—the company may be taking too much risk.

**Tier 1 Capital:** Brokerage firms and other financial firms have multiple tiers of capital deployed, all with varying degrees of risk. The most conservative measure with which to gauge a firm's financial strength is its Tier 1 capital ratio. This is the ratio that many regulators first focus on. The measure is composed of core capital (common stock plus disclosed reserves) divided by a firm's total risk weighted assets (RWA). A higher ratio is safer. When reviewing a possible investment, make sure to understand this metric.

## Industrials

Industrial or cyclical companies represent the true engines of economic growth and are directly tied to the economy. In addition, over the past ten years, most companies are no longer tied only to their domestic economic cycle, but are global in nature. This makes analyzing these companies quite difficult. The right path, however, is to find companies where an overall theme can mitigate a portion of the economic risk. Such investments are referred to as "growth cyclicals" because they have business fundamentals that achieve consistently higher peaks (revenues and earnings) and higher troughs during economic cycles. As you might expect, the best strategy is to buy these stocks at the bottom of an economic cycle (when they seem the most expensive on a P/E basis) and sell at the top (when they seem the cheapest on a P/E basis). Although most of us cannot call market tops and bottoms with accuracy, there are a few metrics we can keep an eye on to help us identify attractive entry and exit points.

**Order Volume:** In addition to traditional valuation metrics, it is important to focus on the quality, trend, and visibility of the order book in an equipment provider or volume growth in a services provider. This metric, often quoted as "book-to-bill," will help provide a view into the future, as well as give an idea of how current business is performing. For example, a weekly publication in the railroad industry called the Railfax Report can be found at http://railfax.transmatch.com. It provides weekly insights into the trends of rail volumes. Order volume is also a great way to research overall economic trends, since economic output is directly tied to rail volume.

**Backlog:** Similar to order flow, understanding where a company's sales come from is very important, since generally we are talking about equipment that takes a long time for delivery. Backlog sales are those which have been placed but not yet delivered. If a company reports strong orders but drew down much of its backlog, one has to be skeptical of the near-term strength of future business.

**Leading Indicators:** Since the bulk of the gains in these stocks come from calling the economic cycle correctly, focusing on economic indicators is important. Particularly useful are the "leading indicators," which are released monthly by the U.S. and foreign governments.

## Technology

Technology stocks are perhaps the most exciting of all stocks due to their close ties with consumers and the potential thrill of hitting a home run with the next Google. Be prepared for huge volatility, large deviations from financial estimates, and rapid competitive changes—these are commonplace to the technology investor. Always remember that your risk is decreased substantially when you can identify significant monopolies, such as Adobe, Apple, Google, or Intel.

We've all heard the saying: the three most important metrics for a real estate purchase are location, location, and location. For technology investments, the three most important metrics are growth, growth, and growth! This sector is not for the faint of heart. Because changes happen fast and today's hot company can be tomorrow's laggard, it is even more important to stick with the companies that exhibit monopolistic and thematic tendencies. In this sector, reduced balance sheet risk, lower dependency on the economy, and products that turn over quite quickly mean the investor's focus has to change to traditional financial statement analysis as well as making sure the companies and products have sustainable competitive advantages.

**Revenue Growth:** Revenue growth, both sequential and year-over-year (YOY), is the most important factor with companies in this sector. High and consistent revenue growth will create an environment for a higher valuation, lower volatility, and consistent profits.

**Margins:** Second only to revenue growth, increasing margins adds leverage to revenue growth and provides strong earnings momentum.

**Valuation:** While it may be tempting to buy a technology stock that trades at a low P/E ratio, more often than not it is cheap for a reason—growth is slow or it has lost its competitive position. It's more important to focus on the P/E relative to the growth rate. If *that* ratio is below 1, it is a positive; if it is above 1, you've got an expensive stock on your hands. However, as mentioned before, many of the strongest performers often trade above their growth rate due to perceived quality. It is important to differentiate between companies that *deserve* a higher valuation and those that do not.

**Orders:** Similar to industrials, many technology companies provide background on the level of orders versus shipments, which can give you incremental information relative to the future.

**Supply Chain:** More than any other sector, technology companies exhibit volatility in between earnings seasons due to data from their supply chains (end users, raw material suppliers, and distributors). The reason is simple: most technology industries have very little backlog or extended visibility. Once you get an order, it ships out almost immediately; thus, near-term data is critical to gaining insight into prospective financials. Make sure you understand customer and vendor concentration, as they are a significant component of your investment due diligence (such as Intel's semiconductors are to Dell computers). Technology companies utilize middlemen to fulfill their orders, so a retailer such as Best Buy (or a distributor like Tech Data) can help you gain insights into the fundamentals of an investment in Intel and Dell.

In addition to the variables mentioned above, each sector within technology has unique characteristics which should be monitored.

**Hardware:** Hardware companies are generally considered commodities, with some exceptions, such as Apple. Margins and orders are key variables to watch.

**Software:** Since most software is sold toward the end of a quarter—when customers demand the largest discounts—it's important to look at DSOs and receivables lines to see how hard they had to push to get the orders. In addition, most software companies have both a sales and a maintenance (services) component; both should be monitored, but new license growth is far more important to future sales than services revenues.

**Services:** Cable, telecom, and other monthly service companies have three additional metrics to pay attention to: (1) new customers, (2) the cost to add new customers (CAC), and (3) the amount of churn (or lost customers) each reporting period.

**Internet:** The Internet poses quite a challenge, as many of the firms resemble "real-world" firms (Amazon and Wal-Mart, for example), but generally, revenue and margin growth should be the focus. Online or Internet firms are going to capture increasing market share from offline firms over time, so they have a "built-in" growth engine. The other important issue is competition; barriers to entry are very low online, so brand name and market share are important.

**Semiconductors:** Semiconductors (chips) are perhaps the most cyclical of all the technology sectors, as they are pervasive and found in almost every device on the planet! In addition, given Moore's Law, these chips, at a minimum, double in performance and halve in cost every twelve to eighteen months, meaning that manufacturers have to sell twice as many every few years just to break even. As a result, new products are continually being brought to market which add value and keep average prices high. Semiconductor companies, including semiconductor equipment companies, trade as much on their order outlook and new product outlook as any other factor. Inventory levels are also important, since products depreciate so rapidly. Pay close attention to whether inventory levels become higher than average, which could signal a potential write-off down the road.

## Consumer

Similar to the technology sector's Intel, Google, and Apple, we all are familiar with Home Depot, Wal-Mart, and Target. These or other powerful consumer-oriented companies should occupy a portion of your portfolio. However, like the technology sector, with the exception of a few large retailers, new product cycles are a key determinant to their success. Other factors to consider include the demographic segment you want exposure to. For example, Wal-Mart clearly caters to value-priced, one-stop-shopping consumers, whereas Tiffany is focused on customers with expensive taste. Below you will see a few factors to consider when looking at a consumer-focused stock.

**Customer Focus and Pricing:** Make sure you understand the type of customer you are investing in, especially when you are considering specialty retailers or companies which focus on specific sectors, such as teens, adults, electronics, furniture, jewelry, etc. In addition, some companies are counter-cyclical (i.e., their results are less affected when the economy is poor), such as Wal-Mart, since consumers increasingly shop for value versus perhaps high-end retailers like Macy's or Saks.

**Monthly Sales:** Many retailers report monthly sales, thus providing an opportunity to get a view into their current sales trends. Be careful to also analyze pricing trends, often called Average Unit Retail (AUR), since if they have to cut prices to drive sales, margins may be lower than expected. Mentioned earlier was a service called www.briefing.com, which provides an analysis of retail sales expectations and results. One of the many benefits of the consumer sector is the ease of due diligence at the customer and competitor level. Visit the stores, ask questions of other customers and employees, and you will be surprised at how open people are and how much knowledge you can gain. Pay attention to pricing, especially around holiday seasons. Are they offering big discounts? These discounts can be data points that will lead to a poor financial report.

**New Stores:** When Starbucks was a young company, its valuation was very high, partly due to a new and unique concept, but also because its geographical penetration was very low, thus providing significant growth and visibility to its revenue stream. Investing in Wal-Mart or McDonald's is very different from a new, hot retailer like Lululemon. Understand where a company stands relative to its penetration opportunity and you will find comfort in perhaps paying a high valuation. Bear in mind that the newer the company, the riskier position it is in, since it is still trying to create a recognizable brand name.

## Energy

While in the technology sector we focus on growth, growth, and growth—in energy, the mantra is price, price, and price! It's the underlying price of energy that really moves this sector. If oil prices are moving down, it's very likely any investment positions related to oil will perform poorly, or flat at best. This is not to say that companies can't differentiate themselves over the long term based on technology, end customer, or segment, but as a rule, make sure you have a concrete directional view and that you track the underlying commodity of your investment. Some factors that will help with your investment include:

**Weekly Production Releases:** The U.S. government releases economic data on a daily basis, but once a week, generally on Wednesdays at 10:30 a.m., the Department of Energy (DOE) releases Oil and Gasoline data. Then, on Thursdays at 10:30 a.m., it releases Natural Gas data. The cable channel CNBC reviews the data each week. Also, generally on Wednesdays, the American Petroleum Institute (API) issues a production release on the oil industry that is watched closely by professionals. Three categories of that data are critical to the energy complex:

i. **Crude Oil Inventories:** Each week a survey is taken and an estimate is projected. As an example, if the actual inventory change (millions of barrels) is greater than expected, producers are building more inventory. Generally, this change would be a bearish signal for oil and related stocks.

ii. **Gasoline Inventories:** Each week a survey is taken and an estimate is projected. As an example, if the actual inventory change (millions of barrels) is greater than expected, producers are building more inventory. Generally, this change would be a bearish signal for gasoline and the stocks that are associated with it.

iii. **Distillate (Heating Oil, Diesel, Jet Fuel) Inventories:** Each week, a survey is taken and an estimate is projected. If the actual inventory change is greater than expected, then producers are building inventory. Generally, this would be a bearish signal for distillates and related stocks.

**Rig Count:** It is intuitive that, as the price of oil or natural gas changes, companies in the production and exploration business will start to spend more or less capital. Making that direct connection is a metric called the Baker Hughes Rig Count, which is released every Friday and serves as an important barometer of current and future business activity for the energy production Industry. The data, which can be found at www.bakerhughes.com, counts the number of active drilling rigs in the U.S and internationally on a weekly and year-over-year basis, thus giving an investor real-time, important, primary data about industry fundamentals.

**Order/Backlog:** This metric is especially important for the Engineering and Services group, companies such as Fluor, Foster Wheeler, and Shaw Group. Similar to industrials, most companies disclose order and backlog guidance. While it is important that a company meet or beat its earnings or revenue estimates, leading indicators—such as order and backlog growth—will be more important to the direction of the stock.

### Other Energy Sectors

**Alternative Energy:** To some extent, the companies involved in this sector, be they solar, wind, biofuels, or energy efficiency, have more in common with the technology sector than the energy industry. Focus in this sector is geared to revenue and earnings growth. At the same time, the stocks will tend to correlate with the price of oil.

**Utilities:** Historically, the utility industry has been more correlated with interest rates, since most have high dividend payouts. Generally, due to high capital intensity and a leveraged business model, when interest rates rise utilities will underperform, and vice versa. In addition, as rates rise, conservative investors will look toward bonds as a substitute. It is not unusual to compare the dividend yield on the utility with that of the overall market.

In recent years, as the energy and power markets have become stressed, the utility sector has morphed into a growth sector. Particularly in the United States, but also in overseas markets, very little power generation capacity has been added over the past twenty years, causing energy shortages in many areas of the world. Combined with old and inefficient infrastructure (i.e., power plants and transmission), this lack of capacity has caused power prices to increase significantly, with no end in sight. While a global recession will likely dampen power demand, there are secular forces at work that lead most to conclude that the price we pay to use power will continue to increase. Each utility in the United States, while regulated in many instances, can re-price its power according to a schedule put forth by the regulatory agencies. When considering an investment in this area, bear this in mind and pay close attention to their "rate case" status, as well as "capacity pricing" events that have recently taken place.

### Basic Resources and Commodities

Commodities and basic resources are very different investment vehicles compared to other sectors. It is beyond the scope of this book to fully prepare the investor for exposure to this sector. However, it is still possible to describe basic attributes of this sector and the variables an investor needs to be aware of to make a more informed, and possibly less risky, investment decision. In addition, because basic industry and commodity companies produce much of the raw materials that fuel our economy, it is important for investors, whether or not they invest in this sector, to review pertinent data as it is revealed to the overall markets.

Since markets and stocks discount future growth, it is critical to pay attention to *any indicator* that might give us an early read on the future. Knowledge of the overall demand and supply balance is a critical investment tool. In many cases, these stocks do not trade on absolute valuation; they trade relative to the underlying commodity to which they are tied. For example, Mosaic, a fertilizer producer, or Nucor, a steel manufacturer, are going to trade with a high correlation to the underlying trends in fertilizer and steel prices. This correlation is distinctly different from other sectors, such as financials, technology, and even industrials.

Since we believe diversification is an important risk management tool, investors should have a portion of their assets allocated to this sector. Similar to the energy sector, the focus is on price, price, and more price.

Generally, an investor who wants exposure to a specific commodity, such as copper, steel, farm grains, or metals, has access to multiple dedicated stocks, as well as specific and broad resource-based exchange-traded funds (ETFs) and indexes. Whether you choose a specific stock or a broad ETF, the performance is likely going to be similar and tied very closely to the underlying commodity trend. Of course, there are other issues associated with purchasing specific stocks:

**Currency (Dollar):** Most commodities are priced in U.S. dollars, meaning that any country that wishes to purchase a barrel of oil, a bushel of corn, or a ton of copper has to convert its currency to U.S. dollars for the purchase. This unique requirement creates a bit of a quagmire, since the currency markets themselves fluctuate significantly on a day-to-day basis. One should be aware that in general, commodities will track *inversely* to the U.S. dollar. As the dollar weakens, it provides an upward bias to commodities, and vice versa, although sometimes this is not the case, since a stronger dollar can mean a better economy, and thus more demand for commodities. This relationship generally occurs because as the dollar weakens, the producers of the oil still need to get the same price for it. Since a declining dollar means they will get less money from converting to their own currency, the price of the barrel of oil has to go up.

**Production:** Revenue growth is a function of both price and volume. Within this sector, production growth dynamics are a key determinant of the value one will place on the company. Companies that have the ability to grow volumes over time will trade at a premium to others, and the stock will also be able to withstand volatility in the underlying price of their product. As an investor, you should own companies that control their production, having the ability to both expand and contract production as warranted by demand and supply fundamentals.

**Production Cost:** Generally, the spoils in the resources and commodities sector go to the lowest-cost producers. Understanding the "cost" of producing a specific unit of the commodity (usually a ton) will provide you with a key insight into where margins and the competitive positioning of a company will trend in the future. This data is often disclosed each financial period and is also helpful with regard to competitive analysis.

**Contracts:** There are two types of contracts to focus on: company- and country-specific. Understanding the contracts of the largest of customers can help give an investor a degree of visibility into the future. In a similar vein, a few commodities take their main cue from country-specific contracts. For example, with the fertilizer potash, each year the market eagerly anticipates the price that China will pay per ton.

**Fertilizer:** A long-term portfolio can benefit from the inclusion of a fertilizer company for a number of reasons, such as strong population growth, growing protein diets in Asia, and a shrinking worldwide base of arable land. All of this data and more point to a world that needs to gain more productivity from existing plantations. Fertilizer is one of the best-understood commodities that can help achieve higher yields. Having said this, fertilizer in and of itself is a commodity, and thus one has to focus as well on the short-term dynamics of price in order to understand how the stock trades. The best pricing source for fertilizer is Green Markets (www.green-markets.com), which reports data every Friday. If you are an institutional investor and plan to invest in the fertilizer sector, the subscription to Green Markets is well worth the price. If you are an individual, the Web site provides breaking news alerts free of charge. *Fertilizer Week* from the CRU Group is another beneficial resource, which also provides useful and timely news free of charge.

The fertilizer markets, be they potash, phosphate, or nitrogen, also trade based on country-specific contracts and farmer fundamentals. Many Asian countries that are dependent upon imports for their needs, such as India and China, will agree to a certain price for a given year, which will set the bar for the fertilizer vendors and Wall Street analysts. Since the farmers are the ultimate end customer for fertilizer, their financial health is also important. Higher corn and soybean prices translate directly into better financial health for the farmers, which then leads to greater fertilizer purchases, as farmers have more profits to allocate to their soil. This cycle will continue until farmers (collectively) have planted too much corn or soybeans, at which time prices reverse, financial health weakens, and fertilizer purchases fall. Once prices fall, planting is curtailed, volumes weaken, and supply and demand come in balance. The cycle starts over again. Understanding this basic cycle will help you when investing in the commodity sector.

**Grains (Corn and Soybeans):** Grain pricing and fundamentals can be found at a number of Web sites, including the Hightower Report (www.futures-research.com), Agweb (www.agweb.com), and Agriculture Online (www.agriculture.com/ag), among others.

Remember the movie *Trading Places* with Eddie Murphy and Dan Aykroyd? How one firm paid to get the USDA's orange juice report early in order to corner the market? Well, with the exception of trying to get inside information, this is mainly how the market works. The U.S. government, on a monthly basis, reports on the quality of the current base of crops and presents any changes in its forecasts. Both farmers and the securities markets will often take their cue from these releases. To get the latest crop data from the USDA, go to www.nass.usda.gov/Newsroom/index.asp. Generally, this information will be reported on the Web sites mentioned above, with a level of review. Pay close attention to this data and it will help your investment performance.

**Base Metals (Copper and Steel):** Base metals are the engine of economic activity on a global basis. Both copper and steel are large components of the industrial and housing complex. While there are supply disruptions from time to time which cause non-economic volatility, generally these commodities represent a barometer of global economic health and should be viewed as such. Copper is much more active than steel as a trading vehicle on the global markets, due to standardized contracts and a more uniform metal. Steel, which comes in many different varieties, while traded, has very little volume associated with it. For our purposes, the only real way for most investors to address the steel markets is through the equity market, whereas one can trade copper easily on a stand-alone basis.

In addition to tracking economic performance (levels of imports, exports, and industrial production) for cues to copper, it's important to also track global inventory levels. Rising inventory levels can portray an economy that is healthy and building, but they can also foretell too much supply and weak economic growth. In addition, China is one of the largest consumers of copper (roughly about one-third of all copper produced) and its buying habits are of great interest to the markets for the underlying commodity and the stocks that track it.

There are generally two types of inventory to track on the London Metals Exchange (LME) and on the Shanghai Exchange. Information about inventory levels and other important related news can be found at many Web sites, such as www.metalprices.com, www.futures-research.com, and www.chinamining.org.

**Steel:** Steel is more regional in nature than copper. Each country has a different situation with respect to its status as a net importer or exporter. The United States is a net importer of steel; thus, U.S. companies that can increase production at low costs have a ready market available. A large majority of steel is produced from scrap metal, which means that focusing on the price of scrap becomes important. This "secular" dynamic in the U.S., while not sheltering steel companies from global economic cycles, does put them in a stronger position to weather downturns. Prices and other information can be found at the Web sites www.steelonthenet.com and www.metalprices.com.

**Precious Metals (Gold and Silver):** Trading in these commodities is not as straightforward as others, and relies as much on global emotions as on raw fundamental information. Neither relies very much on available inventory or mining fundamentals.

**Gold** has historically been viewed from two perspectives: (1) as a hedge against inflation, and (2) as a safety asset. Neither of these two variables relates to the overall demand/supply equation very well; thus, when considering an investment in gold, prepare yourself for the volatility associated with the global macroeconomic trends. Presently, since the dollar is weakening and commodity prices are rising, gold is also on the rise, as concerns of higher commodity prices lead to inflation threats, which lead to more gold purchases. In addition, many turn their attention to gold as an asset when their respective currencies are weakening, since it is a hard asset.

Similarly, **Silver** has a relationship to both inflation and safety, but since it is also used as an industrial metal, economic trends will have a stronger effect on it as compared to gold.

# CHAPTER FOUR

# Be the Investment Manager

## Philosophy and Process are Important, but Discipline is the Key to Success

Unlike some athletes who seem to have been born to win gold medals, nobody comes out of the womb a successful investor. Investing is an acquired skill, and the surest route to uneven performance is to ignore the fundamental underpinnings of any skilled practitioner—philosophy, discipline, and process.

The best managers have a core philosophy that guides their investment choices. They approach all aspects of portfolio management—from identifying investment opportunities to monitoring portfolio holdings to deciding when to sell—with a rigorous discipline verging on obsession. And they utilize the same *measurable* process each time they make an investment, both to identify successful approaches and to learn from unsuccessful ones.

The philosophy of the Monopoly Method is that a focus on companies with true monopolies or significant monopolistic tendencies will produce, over time, strong investment returns coupled with moderated risk. It is also the most efficient and productive way to choose stocks for those who are not full-time investment professionals.

But a sound philosophy is useless without rigorous discipline. A discipline is a systematic approach to learning as much as is reasonably possible about a potential investment, and staying informed about that investment once you own it.

There are a number of crucial sources of information about the state of a company's business. Not all are of equal value, however. Testimony from a company's customers, for example, is far more valuable than that of a Wall Street analyst.

A disciplined approach to information gathering will hit five major touch-points of any company's business. Below, from left to right, in increasing order of importance, is the Discipline System of the Monopoly Method.

**Figure 4.1 The Discipline System**

| Level 1 | Level 2 | Level 3 | Level 4 | Level 5 |
|---------|---------|---------|---------|---------|
| Analyst | Company | Consultant | Channel | Customer / Competitor |
| Brokerage Firm | Company Management | Industry Expert | Suppliers or Distributors | Specific Customer or Competitor |

You might be thinking, "Shouldn't interacting with the company be farther to the right?" It's a natural question, but the answer is no. Why?

First and foremost, management teams are biased, and are likely to give you a positive spin on any news whatsoever, be it truly good or bad. That's only natural—the best entrepreneurs are optimists—but it also degrades the value of any offered "insight" into the state of the business.

Secondly, since the implementation of Regulation Fair Disclosure in the wake of the accounting scandals at Enron, Worldcom, and elsewhere, the value of data points from any company has been marginalized. Why is that? Because now *everybody* knows what a company has to say—it's illegal for disclosure to come in any other way. The best edge in the stock market comes from seeing or hearing something *before* everybody else does. In our discipline system, the further to the right your data comes from, the more "proprietary" it is.

## Level 1 – Analyst

While Wall Street's influence on the direction of stocks has lessened over the years, its analysts can still move prices, especially in the short term. Why? Because they bring a singular focus on and perspective into the companies they cover. Wall

Street analysts speak with management teams on a regular basis, and while significant disclosures are supposed to be made to everyone, it is still possible that an analyst has gained important insights from a recent call with a company, consultant, channel, or customer. It's important to try to get as timely a read on information flow as possible, and while it's a tall task to think you can follow every single analyst covering every single stock you own, you should consider picking your favorites and staying on top of their periodic comments and upgrades or downgrades.

Of course, as often as not, an upgrade or downgrade is a *result* of the news, not the news itself. When it was announced in late April 2010 that Goldman Sachs might be under investigation by federal prosecutors, a number of analysts downgraded the stock upon hearing the news. The horse had already left the barn, however, with the stock already down nearly 10 percent in a single day.

So ask the question: why (and when) was the last upgrade or downgrade made, and what was the reasoning? And don't ignore those with whom you do not agree. It's important to understand both the bullish and bearish views on your possible or current investment. Briefing.com is an excellent and inexpensive source for analyst data.

Of equal if not greater importance: understanding the earnings "expectations" or "whisper numbers" being projected by Wall Street. Stocks are always pricing in some form of expectations, especially as they head into quarterly earnings reporting season, and they may not be those you can find as "consensus" estimates.

When a stock trades down after a company has reported earnings that beat estimates, even if the beat was "high quality," the reason is usually that the stock was priced for a bigger beat and the "whisper" numbers were higher.

As an individual investor, it is not always easy to figure out what expectations are, but a good rule of thumb is to look at the performance of the stock prior to the financial report, as well as its valuation. If performance has moved up considerably or the valuation is high (relative to history), there is a high probability that the expectations are for a beat and raise—meaning, the company will beat the estimates and analysts will raise earnings guidance for the next quarter.

## Level 2 – Company

Communication with prospective or current portfolio companies falls into two categories—one-way or two-way.

One-way communication comes in the form of webcasts or conference calls companies provide to investors as a method to disclose and discuss financial results, corporate strategy, or other information. Wall Street analysts are on every call, asking important questions so as to provide their clients with an update based on knowledge gained. Most of these conference calls are accessible to the public and should be listened to in real time or as soon as possible thereafter. Scheduling these events is easy, especially if you use a system such as briefing.com.

The other method, two-way communication, is a privilege usually accorded to professional investors but which is not entirely out of the realm of consideration for individual shareholders. The gatekeeper to such communication is the investor relations manager.

Conversations with management are tough to come by, so it's important to stay focused on extracting the most valuable information possible if you happen to find yourself in one. Because stock prices tend to be a function of investor estimates of future cash flows, the majority of your questioning should concern directional movement in revenues and margins, both on an absolute basis but also relative to expectations. For example, you might ask why gross margins were flat this quarter and what factors will contribute to their rise or fall over the next few quarters.

Interacting with management is one of the most challenging aspects of the professional investment process, but with time, patience, and practice you will find enormous benefits. In addition to the knowledge and satisfaction gained by meeting and speaking with very talented and experienced people, you will increase your investment perception, and likely, your results. Much more about interaction with management teams is discussed in the advanced knowledge section.

## Level 3 – Consultants/Expert Networks

Consultants are similar to Wall Street analysts, but their customers are not only investors. Just as you are seeking intelligence on a company's products, prospects, and competition, so, too, are companies themselves, and consultants are often called in to tell companies things even *they* don't know about their own business.

Expert networks, which are just what they sound like—networks of experts who are tapped (and paid) for their insight about a particular industry or product—are often populated by former employees of the companies they are talking about. Thus, their knowledge can be highly valuable.

While the product of consulting firms can be expensive, it can also be worth every penny. It usually includes information on three aspects of a business.

1. **Structure of Market:** Consultants spend a great deal of time trying to understand how a market is structured, its growth potential, and its maturity level. They will help you gain the knowledge needed to decide whether your growth estimates or those of Wall Street have a high probability of success. In addition, they provide an independent review about the industry you are considering investing in.

2. **Competitive Landscape:** Understanding the competitive positioning of a company is perhaps the single biggest problem most investors face. Any firm can get blindsided by a competitor bringing out a better product that captures market share. It is reasonable that you will spend less time conducting due diligence on competitors than on your own holdings, but consultants can offer insightful reviews of the competitive landscape.

3. **Management Depth:** Since most consultants come from the industry they are covering, they often bring to the table an understanding of the specific individuals involved. Consultants who have worked at companies themselves can provide insight into the work ethic, long-term performance, and intellectual capacity of their management teams.

While many consultants are priced at levels which are not cost-effective for individuals—firms such as CognoLink, Coleman Research Group, DeMatteo Monness, Gerson Lehrman Group, Guidepoint Global, Seeking Experts, Tribeca Insights, and Vista Research—there do exist lower-priced services which connect experts electronically. LinkedIn, which is comprised of roughly forty million business members, is a great example of a moderately priced expert network. In addition, a search on the Internet, be it blogs or other sites, can often reveal important and relevant information. There are many Web sites specifically devoted to the particular sectors or niches to which many companies provide products.

In some cases, the more expensive firms are also moving toward transactional billing. This means that individuals might use their services on an ad hoc basis without incurring monthly retainer fees. One of the most exciting new networks is www.zintro.com. This network, started in 2009, provides efficiency by employing an auction-type format. (Think Priceline for information!) Investors can bid at a price that makes sense for them.

Whether you are an investment professional or an individual, spending a few extra dollars on an expert network or conducting additional industry work can help you increase your investment success.

## Level 4 – Supply Channel and "Food Chain"

All investors are familiar with the experience of waking up one day to find a stock holding down significantly, without any apparent news out of the company itself. There could be many reasons for such—a large shareholder deciding to dump its holdings, for example—but one of the most frequent is that there is "indirect" news from one of the company's customers or from vendors who supply products to it.

The group of companies both upstream and downstream from another company—its suppliers and its customers—is referred to as its "food chain" or its "channel." And it acts as a real-time and potentially leading indicator, sometimes allowing investors to make critical decisions *before* a company reports a positive or negative financial result. In other words, the channel can act as a check to your investment rationale, providing evidence that either supports or nullifies your thesis.

There are a number of ways investors can monitor the "food chain" or supply channel, but there are four that you should focus on to help separate the noise from the signals:

**Suppliers.** Every company purchases raw materials to make its products, whether it's in a service or manufacturing business. Monitoring the suppliers of the key materials can provide unique insights into a current or prospective investment.

**Distributors.** Many companies sell through intermediaries that are also publicly traded. Monitoring these companies can provide useful insights to all investors.

**Corporate Customers.** Monitoring inventory levels at a customer of a company gives an investor critical information about the demand/supply environment. It follows that if a large customer has ample supply of a product, it is less likely to order more.

**Retail Stores.** Many firms sell their products at retail stores that are also public companies. By tracking the health of retail purchases, one can get a great feel for the prospects of his or her portfolio holdings.

There are a few services that can provide a good read on the supply chain. The best is Connexiti (which was acquired by Bloomberg), which publishes data on over two hundred thousand companies globally. Connexiti is a very robust product, and is mainly used by institutional or professional investors.

The individual investor can still build his or her own supply chain model with information from company filings such as 10Q and 10K reports, both of which break out key customers and suppliers. The following chart shows all the companies that do significant business with router maker Cisco Systems. It looks hairy, but once you have taken the time to build the model, the updates are relatively easy. The knowledge one gains over time with this process can provide powerful insight, in addition to saving you from getting blindsided.

### Figure 4.2 Supply Chain Chart

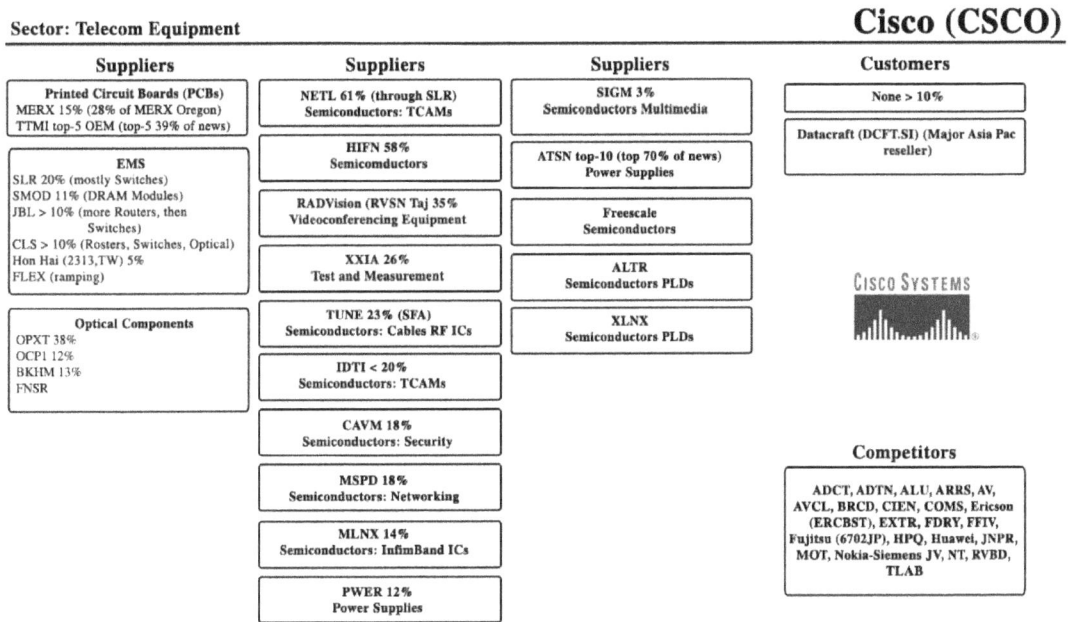

| Sector: Telecom Equipment | | | Cisco (CSCO) |
|---|---|---|---|
| **Suppliers** | **Suppliers** | **Suppliers** | **Customers** |
| Printed Circuit Boards (PCBs)<br>MERX 15% (28% of MERX Oregon)<br>TTMI top-5 OEM (top-5 39% of news) | NETL 61% (through SLR)<br>Semiconductors: TCAMs | SIGM 3%<br>Semiconductors Multimedia | None > 10% |
| | HIFN 58%<br>Semicomductors | ATSN top-10 (top 70% of news)<br>Power Supplies | Datacraft (DCFT.SI) (Major Asia Pac reseller) |
| EMS<br>SLR 20% (mostly Switches)<br>SMOD 11% (DRAM Modules)<br>JBL > 10% (more Routers, then Switches)<br>CLS > 10% (Rosters, Switches, Optical)<br>Hon Hai (2313,TW) 5%<br>FLEX (ramping) | RADVision (RVSN Taj 35%<br>Videoconferencing Equipment | Freescale<br>Semiconductors | |
| | XXIA 26%<br>Test and Measurement | ALTR<br>Semiconductors PLDs | CISCO SYSTEMS |
| Optical Components<br>OPXT 38%<br>OCP1 12%<br>BKHM 13%<br>FNSR | TUNE 23% (SFA)<br>Semiconductors: Cables RF ICs | XLNX<br>Semiconductors PLDs | |
| | IDTI < 20%<br>Semiconductors: TCAMs | | |
| | CAVM 18%<br>Semiconductors: Security | | **Competitors** |
| | MSPD 18%<br>Semiconductors: Networking | | ADCT, ADTN, ALU, ARRS, AV,<br>AVCL, BRCD, CIEN, COMS, Ericson<br>(ERCBST), EXTR, FDRY, FFIV,<br>Fujitsu (6702JP), HPQ, Huawei, JNPR,<br>MOT, Nokia-Siemens JV, NT, RVBD,<br>TLAB |
| | MLNX 14%<br>Semiconductors: InfimBand ICs | | |
| | PWER 12%<br>Power Supplies | | |

Source: Citigroup 2007 report

## Level 5 – Customers and Competitors

The fifth level is the most important of all: the customers (competitors) that keep your portfolio holding in or out of business. Customer or competitor relationships, of course, have to be taken in the context of both the size and quality of the relationship. Generally, if a customer accounts for greater than 10 percent of sales, pay attention. Customer concentration is reported annually in a company's 10K (filed with the Securities and Exchange Commission), or can be found through research on the Internet. Knowledge of a customer's or a competitor's performance—*especially if it reports its financials before your holding does*—could foretell the financial report of your holding. In this way, you've gotten out in front to see if the company will meet, miss, or beat expectations.

### Discipline Is *THE* Glue

A strong discipline is the glue that holds the Monopoly Method together. A strong discipline is also the engine that will drive you to the right themes and monopolies—and it is the engine that helps you decide what scores to enter for your process (which will be discussed in chapter 6). Without an effective discipline, there is no Monopoly Method and no way to both replicate and measure your performance, which in the end is needed to help you learn and grow as an investor.

Along with a structured discipline, a daily or weekly routine is advisable. An example of a typical day is presented in the advanced knowledge section. Routine and structure will help you utilize your time efficiently, since most of us have precious little extra time as it is.

# CHAPTER FIVE

# Building the Monopoly Philosophy
## The Right Place at the Right Time

Way back before hedge funds took over Wall Street, one manager stood above them all. His name was Peter Lynch, and he worked for Fidelity Investments. Lynch's success at Fidelity is legendary. When he took over the Magellan Fund in 1977, it had $18 million in assets. When he left in 1990, it was over $14 billion.

Mr. Lynch is perhaps most famous for his saying, "Invest in what you know." It's a bedrock insight that should be a component of every investor's strategy to this day. Most part-time investment non-professionals do not have time to pore over financial reports, speak with companies, or track important data; however, most of us work in a profession in which we have garnered some level of expertise. This expertise can be used to achieve better investment results.

The downside to this approach is the concept of over-concentration. Much of your future net worth is tied to your ability to keep your job, which means you're already significantly invested in your industry. To then double down by investing most of your portfolio in the stocks of companies you work for or compete with has its attendant risks. Just ask anyone who worked for Enron, Lehman Brothers, Bear Stearns, AIG, Worldcom and had his or her 401(k) tied up in stock in the company.

The tension between expertise and over-concentration is real, and it gets to the core of the following questions: How do we get the most efficiency out of our time conducting research into our portfolio holdings? And can we really achieve a higher probability of a successful investment outcome without having personal experience and expertise?

The answer is yes. Advantage comes from the ability to measure and change—and the only way to measure and change is to practice the same philosophy, discipline, and process time after time after time. A good baseball player learns over time how to adjust his approach, but he can't make changes unless he has a framework in which he works. Only a lucky few are switch-hitters. Most of us have to stick with left- or right-handed, and to try to get better over time.

There are two factors that lead to an increased probability of higher returns in any investment portfolio. You need to be in the *right place* at the *right time*. Sounds easy enough, but look at your current portfolio. Is it positioned for both?

### The Right Time = Thematic Investing

Most investment decisions have some thematic elements to them, but our investment portfolios often fall short of a true thematic approach. For example, Apple Inc. has been a core holding for my hedge fund, Rock Crest Capital, since my wife Cecilia bought one of the first iPods several years ago. She was a general consumer with little knowledge of technology, yet she had found a product that truly met her needs. To me, this screamed mass-market appeal—it meant that the iPod as a product had significant potential. Whether or not Apple Inc. was a great stock to own required further work. I needed to understand what particular problem or lifestyle issue was being solved by the iPod. In short, what was the "theme" of the iPod purchase, and how big and proprietary could the opportunity be for Apple Inc.? In addition, how did the iPod fare versus other products of the same ilk?

Back then, Apple Inc. was not the star performer you see today. The company was viewed as a "has-been" in the PC wars, with high costs and low market share, and while it had a cadre of devotees, it wasn't a company on the move. Thinking of my wife as a Level 5 customer (from the discipline system), I was able to back into a theme (stocks don't always have to come from themes; often it can be the reverse) around which to base my thinking: *the third screen*. Most of us have TVs. Most of us use computers. And, up until a few years ago, most of us had a third screen—the mobile phone—but it was mainly for voice communication. What if Apple was introducing a third screen into our lives for multimedia use that was easy to use? Of course, simple logic and math could get us to astounding numbers if the theme was correct. Developing themes acts as a check and balance to your ideas and helps you develop confidence and stronger investment performance.

Consider Apple Inc. If a significant portion of the mobile phone market added multimedia functionality—and as of today, it already has—you could foresee a market opportunity of 330 million phones a year, or 25 percent of the total market of 1.3 billion phones (which you can find out by searching the Internet). And if Apple could grab a 25 percent share—today it's over 40 percent in the USA—then it could sell over 80 million iPhones per year. At $400 per phone—today, it's over $600—that equates to over $32 billion in annual sales for the iPhone alone. Apple's total sales in 2008 were about $33 billion. That gives you some perspective about what can happen when a company is in the right place—iPod plus iPhone—at the right time. In this case, we're talking about the deployment of the third screen. Not only does this type of simple analysis help provide the framework for an investment, it also can give an investor the confidence to hold on to the stock during volatile periods or come back to it quickly when the markets recover.

The idea behind the philosophy of the Monopoly Method is to populate your investment portfolio with companies such as Apple Inc. But to get to the right place, first we have to identify the right time or the right themes. Once we identify those, we can look for companies such as Apple in which to make our investments.

There are thousands of publicly traded companies out there, so it's imperative to bring focus to your selection discipline. Thematic investing—that is, selecting investments that benefit from major technological, economic, demographic, or societal changes—will provide that focus. It will also provide diversification, in the process lowering overall risk and simultaneously giving your portfolio a higher probability of sustained investment success.

Trends or themes create winners and losers. For example, old-line mobile communication companies such as Motorola or Nokia have not kept up with new emerging trends and have suffered severely at the expense of Research in Motion and Apple. Telephone and data network companies such as Lucent and Nortel lost their way as new Internet and networking companies like Cisco Systems addressed customer needs by providing robust, low-cost, and distributed network equipment. The list goes on and on. There are always secular shifts happening in the global economy, and by aligning your portfolio with these shifts, your investment performance will improve. Deployment of capital to high- growth markets creates opportunity for a lengthy period of profit growth, which ultimately leads to better stock performance. These companies have greater visibility and a stronger growth profile, which ultimately lead to lower risk.

While we will discuss multiple themes in this chapter, take this time to look at your current portfolio and assess the themes that are present. A larger and more thoughtful project is to take the time to develop five to ten themes that you believe have strong prospects for sustained growth over the next few years. Your goal is to align your portfolio with these themes over time.

## The Right Place = The Monopoly Approach

There are two elements to your philosophy: first, find the themes to invest in—the right time—and second, put your money to work in the companies that are benefiting the most from this theme—the right place. The idea is to create layers of probabilities. Your odds of success increase by investing in the right theme, and then increase even more by investing in the right companies.

Monopolies or companies that have monopolistic tendencies have unfair advantages for one reason or another. These advantages give them a competitive boost over their industry peers and generally lead to high and growing market share, stronger financial metrics, the power to price products at a premium, and the ability not only to weather a downturn more successfully, but also to make the strategic decisions necessary in that downturn which position them to be even stronger during the next upturn. A perfect example of this phenomenon is Cisco Systems, which has executed magnificently under the leadership of John Chambers since 1991. Not only has its market share increased over time in its core markets, but it has grown to dominate multiple end markets, often taking advantage of a challenging economic environment to move into a new sector and apply its strategy all over again.

Once you've identified the themes you feel strongly about, it is time to find those companies that will benefit disproportionately from the rest. For example, if you believe the world will run short on food as we add another three billion or so people to our planet in the next few decades, or that global climate change will create serious water shortages in the future, then a by-product of those themes is an age-old question asked for these modern times: how do we make more food? The answer can come in a variety of ways, but certainly among them is to increase the output of the crops we plant. One way to do that is through increased fertilizer use. Another is enhancing the seeds planted. Potash and Mosaic are dominant fertilizer providers. Monsanto dominates the seed creation business. As you can see, by focusing on a theme and the monopolies within, you can identify *potential* investments quickly. Once you've identified the opportunities, you can use the discipline and process systems to conduct due diligence and decide whether they should be a part of your portfolio.

We are looking for companies that are either true monopolies or have significant monopolistic tendencies. Attributes to focus on include:

A.  High and growing market share, which should be *significantly higher* than the next competitor.

B.  Better financial metrics than others in the industry. A higher return on capital deployed will allow them to continue to dominate and expand market share.

C.  Look for a sustained advantage that others cannot have or have had difficulty replicating. For example, Apple and the iPhone, Potash's ownership of potash mining sites, and Boeing's dominance in the new airplane market. While there will always be short-term periods where they and other stocks will underperform, over the long term these unfair advantages will lead to better investment returns at lower levels of risk.

You will be surprised at just how many strong themes and monopolies emerge once you set your mind to it. What follows are some of the more interesting macro themes of today and the companies that dominate them. This is by no means an exhaustive list.

### Potential "Right Place at the Right Time" Companies

1.  **Aerospace Industry** – We are witnessing one of the most significant changes to the way airplanes are being designed, built, and tested.

a.  Lighter weight materials such as carbon composites and titanium are replacing aluminum and other metals as the material of choice for structural components. The results are huge weight savings, which directly affect operating cost elements such as fuel usage.

b.  Enhancements to engine designs have brought forth significantly better fuel efficiency.

c.  The airplane design and construction process, which historically was highly secretive and in-house, has shifted to an outsourced model. Never have we seen such a massive shift in the way airplanes are brought to market.

d.  The extreme growth of emerging economies in Latin America, the Middle East, India, and China is creating acceleration in airline demand growth, as many new economies benefit from a growing and richer middle class used to flying.

### Monopolistic Companies Which Benefit Include:

**A.** **Boeing (BA)** – Designer of the all-composite 787 airliner. While the introduction of the plane was significantly delayed, was over budget, and is still undergoing testing, the advantages from this design mark a truly historic change in aircraft manufacture.

**B.** **General Electric (GE)** – While GE participates in many aerospace businesses, it is dominant in the jet engine segment.

**C.** **Hexcel (HXL)** – This advanced composites and specialty metals manufacturer is one of a few companies that dominate this growing sector.

**D.** **Precision Castparts (PCP)** – A manufacturer of complex structural components and a prime beneficiary of the move toward design and construction outsourcing.

2. **Oil and Gas Infrastructure** – Existing high-production fields have seen volumes peaking; emerging countries are seeing economic expansion, and population growth could exceed 50 percent over the next thirty to forty years. These factors will likely lead to high energy prices and significant exploration and development infrastructure growth.

a. Development costs for energy exploration are increasing significantly, both on an absolute basis and on a per-barrel basis. This factor leads to high growth for firms which provide technological and productivity enhancements.

b. The industry is undergoing a significant shift to offshore and/or deepwater drilling where larger fields are available.

c. New natural gas technologies such as horizontal drilling have increased production yields as well as expanded the geographical footprint available for exploration.

**Monopolistic Companies Which Benefit Include:**

**A.   Cameron (CAM) and FMC Technologies (FTI)** – Oil services equipment manufacturers with dominant positions in offshore equipment. Both have strong technology platforms which are being adopted throughout the industry.

**B.   Fluor Corporation (FLR)** – Leading engineering and services company with significant exposure to the oil and gas sector.

**C.   Ion Geophysical (IO)** – Manufacturer of complex energy exploration software and services.

**D.   Schlumberger (SLB)** – Dominant oil services equipment provider. Also provides exploration software and services.

3.   **Power Infrastructure** – Existing global power infrastructures are very old, extremely inefficient, isolated from each other, and centered close to urban environments. As we enter an age marked by ever-increasing digital information, environmental concerns, and geopolitical strife, the power and transmission infrastructure will undergo the most significant upgrade since it was created almost one hundred years ago.

a.   The power infrastructure in the United States is exceedingly complex and fragmented, with almost twenty thousand transmission substations managed by over three thousand entities! Approximately 70 percent of the transformers, transmission lines, and circuit breakers are at least twenty-five years old and are underpowered given today's Internet and power needs. In general, we are still using electro-mechanical devices versus state-of-the-art microprocessor solutions.

b.   The electric power grid has very little real-time ability to manage power at a residential or commercial level. Simply put, it is extremely inefficient. Because of this liability, high-cost standby power sources are necessary. Today, there are many companies and a few dominant players which help address the real-time information and management needs of the utility, residential, and commercial customers. Longer term, the power community will move to use the Internet as a robust communications and management tool.

c.   New renewable power sources, such as wind turbines, solar, biomass, and biofuels, are highly location dependent and often are located in areas without sufficient transmission capacity. Estimates for the cost to extend and increase the power of our current transmission infrastructure can run up to $2 million per mile.

d.  Even within traditional energy sources, such as gas, coal, and nuclear, major shifts are occurring. Presently, about 50 percent of the power in the United States comes from coal, but as environmental concerns heat up there will be a shift to cleaner natural gas and nuclear energy.

e.  New nuclear plant designs will usher in a major renaissance, as they are much safer and more efficient, produce cost-effective energy, have zero carbon emission, and will reprocess spent fuel.

### Monopolistic Companies Which Benefit Include:

A.  **ABB Limited (ABB)** – Provides power and automation technologies and is a dominant global transmission and distribution equipment supplier.

B.  **Quanta Services (PWR)** – Provides specialized transmission and distribution services to electric utilities which are managing and expanding their transmission infrastructure.

C.  **Shaw Group (SHAW)** – Engineering and services vendor with an ownership interest in the most popular new nuclear plant technology.

D.  **Itron (ITRI)** – Leading utility demand and efficiency products vendor.

E.  **Florida Power & Light (FPL)** – Leading renewable energy utility based in Florida.

4.  **Renewable Energy** – New sources of energy production are becoming competitively priced with traditional sources such as coal, natural gas, and nuclear. In addition, the environmental and geopolitical consequences of current energy sources are creating significant opportunities for renewable forms of production.

a.  Major legislative and incentive efforts are being put forth globally to usher in a new era based on renewable forms of energy. These efforts will likely continue, providing a substantial lift to the companies in this area.

b. Solar technology, in all its various forms (PV, CST, CSP) can only compete today with peak utility rates in select geographies (California). By 2012, however, solar is on track to be truly competitive in a high proportion of geographies where the environment is suitable.

c. Presently, wind turbines are the main source of renewable energy production globally. After years of stagnation, with industry growth mainly relying on more powerful turbines, new technologies, companies, and processes are evolving at a breakneck pace. In addition, complex incentive schemes, which in the past have created boom-and-bust cycles, have been replaced by a growing and stable array of incentive packages. Given the complexity of designing, building, and servicing thousand-foot-tall towers, a few companies have risen to the top and will likely have many years of prosperous growth.

d. High levels of carbon dioxide ($CO_2$) are considered to be the main cause of global warming. As a result, over the next several years, it's likely that global legislation will be enacted that will require extreme penalties for those producing high levels of this gas. A mechanism used to combat $CO_2$ growth, called "cap and trade," will usher in a multi-hundred-billion-dollar market in carbon credits. Two main investment themes will emerge:

   I   Companies that create carbon offset projects (methane gas removal from a waste facility) or that utilize carbon neutral energy production technology (such as wind and solar).
   II  Service-based companies that are either carbon heavy (such as a coal utility) or light (such as nuclear companies).

e. Bio-energy, or fuel produced from materials with biological properties, such as ethanol in its many forms, biodiesel, algae, and biomass-derived electricity, continue to advance toward large-scale, efficient production. While many obstacles and political challenges remain, energy production from biological sources will be a significant part of the renewable energy landscape. The investable landscape within bio-energy is very diverse, given the very large and broad supply chain, including crop producers and traders (corn, soybean, palm), agricultural equipment, and bio-energy producers.

**Monopolistic Companies Which Benefit Include:**

**A. Solar: First Solar (FSLR), Sunpower (SPWRA), Suntech (STP), Meyer Burger Technology AG (MBTN)** – While the solar food chain is quickly approaching commoditization, a few companies have established defensible competitive positions, forming technically rich, high-volume, integrated, and low-cost operations.

B.  **Vestas Wind Systems (VWDRY)** – Leading high-volume and technically rich wind turbine vendor.

C.  **Exelon (EXE) and Florida Power & Light (FPL)** – Leading U.S.-based nuclear- and wind-dominated utilities likely to benefit when carbon legislation is enacted.

D.  **Potash (POT), Mosaic (MOS), and Bunge (BG)** – Leading global agricultural service, fertilizer, and trading providers which will benefit from the growth of bio-based fuels.

5.  **Water and Waste Management Infrastructure and Services** – In 1996, World Bank VP Ismail Serageldin said, "If the wars of this century were fought over oil, the wars of the next century will be fought over water." While many might disagree with this statement, water scarcity could be the looming problem of our time. Water use is growing at over twice the rate of population growth, supply is static at best, and one-third of the world lives in water-stressed areas. Taken in combination with the severe pollution problems in China, water technology, management and efficiency will take center stage during the next ten years.

a.  According to the UN World Water Development Report, over 70 percent of water consumption comes from the agricultural sector. Remarkably, the UN's World Water Assessment Program says that almost 60 percent of irrigation water is wasted! Farmers use fresh water to irrigate their crops inefficiently. New technologies such as drip irrigation, as well as other high-efficiency measures, will be needed to reduce this problem.

b.  Water management is still nationalized in most places. Approximately 5 percent of Asia and 35 percent of the United States is managed privately, opening up a potentially large opportunity for private capital to increase productivity.

c.  As water scarcity increases and prices for water increase, other forms of water creation such as desalination will gain hold. For example, desalination costs have dropped significantly over the past few years and will likely continue down a steep curve.

d. Global water infrastructure is old, has high ongoing maintenance costs, and is extraordinarily inefficient. In some low-income countries, losses due to theft, poor infrastructure, and inefficient metering can represents 50 to 60 percent of water supplied, with a global average estimated at 35 percent. The EPA notes that only 60 percent of water pipes in the United States are in acceptable condition, versus 87 percent in 1980.

e. As water supplies tighten and prices rise, especially in emerging countries, grain imports will replace water use, since agriculture is the largest component of water demand.

f. Wastewater, which comes from both residential and commercial enterprises, is historically treated at large-scale plants, consuming significant energy resources. Waste-to-Energy (WTE) technologies addressing water waste have matured and can provide a positive net energy balance, thus creating a multi-billion-dollar market globally.

g. Increased emphasis on a sustainable environment will accelerate efficient waste management and recycling technologies globally. For example, only 29 percent of solid waste is recycled in the United States, and less in emerging countries.

### Monopolistic Companies Which Benefit Include:

A. **Veolia Environment (VE)** – Veolia operates water management systems globally and is particularly well positioned to benefit from the growing trend toward water management privatization.

B. **Tetra Tech Inc. (TTEK)** – Provides specialty management and technical consulting services to the resource management sector, with particular expertise in water infrastructure and desalination-related projects.

C. **Monsanto (MON)** – Leading specialty seed developer, with particular expertise developing seeds that increase yields in resource-challenged environments.

D. **Potash Corporation (POT)** – As the population grows and water supplies tighten, crop yields will need to increase significantly. Specialty fertilizer such as potash will be used in increasing amounts and is only available through a few companies globally.

E. **Covanta Holding (CVA)** – Leading waste-to-energy and waste efficiencies provider.

F. **Pentair (PNR)** – This diversified manufacturer has a large concentration in water-related products, with a strong presence in the filtration, pump, and waste management segment.

6. **Advanced Materials, Metals, and Commodities** – Three factors are leading to significant resource management issues globally, as well as creating notable demand for advanced materials. The emergence of Brazil, Russia, India, and China (BRIC) as significant economies with a growing middle class, a global population that will likely increase more than 50 percent in the next twenty to thirty years, and a planet that is focused on sustainable management are all combining to create a stressful environment for traditional resources.

a. Demand for increased fuel and infrastructure efficiency is bringing about new materials, such as carbon fiber, that are both lighter and stronger than their predecessors.

b. Increased price volatility of resources will shift the competitive dynamics to those companies which are fully integrated and can manage price risk efficiently.

c. Steel capacity will tighten as a recovery gains hold, since zero capacity has been added globally since 1997.

d. Tighter regulatory and environmental standards are raising operational costs globally, which will continue to stress the importance of low-cost operations and resource efficiency.

### Monopolistic Companies Which Benefit Include:

A. **Nucor (NUE)** – U.S. steel producers are particularly well positioned, since the U.S. is a net importer of steel, and Nucor is in an enviable position based on its low-cost expansionary model.

B. **Freeport McMoran (FCX)** – Dominant position in both copper and gold mining, both of which are constrained globally.

**C. ArcelorMittal (MT)** – Leading globally integrated steel manufacturer with control over its raw material resources.

**D. Dynamic Materials (BOOM)** – Using an innovative technique, Dynamic Materials produces higher-strength metals versus conventional methods at similar or lower costs.

5. **Technology Sector** – Technological progress is accelerating at a fast pace, giving rise to numerous important and global opportunities.

a. Mobile devices have reached critical performance and networking thresholds, driving demand for smaller form factors, broadband access, and high-quality video.

b. Consumer lifestyles have been dramatically altered digitally, with higher-performance viewing/display technology, richer video and gaming performance, and, increasingly, access to high-quality, low-cost multimedia content via the Internet in the family space (TV room).

c. A new capital spending cycle for communications equipment is occurring and is driven by voice/data/video broadband network expansions and emerging market infrastructure growth.

d. Internet technologies have matured and are driving a rapid shift from traditional structures to online structures.

### Monopolistic Companies Which Benefit Include:

**A. Adobe Systems (ADBE)** – With the 2005 acquisition of Macromedia, Adobe has solidified its stature as the premier provider of digital media and document management tools. As more firms embrace and extend their presence on the Internet, Adobe will be there to provide Web site, graphics, video, collaboration, editing, and mobile development tools.

**B. Autodesk (ADSK)** – In a similar fashion to Adobe, Autodesk has locked up the software design market for architectural and mechanical design, geographic information systems, and mapping and visualization applications. As our planet focuses more intently on the environment, in combination with the dynamic growth in China and other emerging markets, Autodesk is positioned to enjoy sustained growth.

**C. Google (GOOG)** – With over 65 percent market share and one of the most recognizable brands on the planet, Google is positioned perfectly to benefit from the shift of advertising and search functions to the Internet. In addition, as video content continues to flourish, the company's acquisition of YouTube will aid in expansion of its revenue streams.

**D. Apple (AAPL)** – With its low penetration of PCs globally, and a new and exciting mobile product (iPhone/iPad), Apple is positioned to enjoy multiple years of sustained growth.

**E. American Tower (AMT)** – Owns, operates, and rents space on its wireless towers. As the wireless industry continues to grow, and as the breadth of technologies expands on these networks, they will be in constant need for additional bandwidth and better coverage.

This is a short list, but it gives you a framework for creating your own thematic and monopolistic style. When you focus on companies that are in the right place at the right time, your probability of a successful investment increases substantially. Keep your philosophy focused on these types of companies and you will have long-term success.

# CHAPTER SIX

# Tying a Strong Philosophy and Discipline Together

## Introducing a Powerful yet Simple Process for Investment Selection, Management, and Trading

As in many disciplines, consistency is an absolute requirement for long-term success in investing. Anyone can pick a winner once. Or twice.

A consistent philosophy will keep you focused on the kinds of companies that are more likely to produce solid returns. The Monopoly Method utilizes one such philosophy.

A consistent discipline will keep you focused on what's important about those companies that your philosophy identifies. Separating the noise from the signal is an ongoing job with any investment candidates—as well as any investments in the portfolio.

Across most industries, you will find that most successful people discover a formula and stick to it—only changing if they have been proven incorrect by a system of measurement. That's the point of a system in the first place—to have the ability to measure your results and make adjustments.

That's where process comes in. It's where the rubber meets the road in investing. It's how you answer the most important questions of all, namely:

1. How do I decide the right time to initiate a position?
2. How do I decide between multiple investment selections?

3. How do I determine which investments should be more heavily weighted in my portfolio?
4. How do I decide when to sell or take profits?

One definition of process is "a series of actions, changes, or functions bringing about a result." Every investor should be able to clearly identify his or her process, repeat it with each possible investment, and track its results. With measurement, your ability to adjust your process to meet your investment goals increases. This is what separates successful money managers from dilettantes.

A rigorous process will also allow you to fight your instincts, such as buying more of a position after it has gone up. If you thought a stock was a good buy at ten dollars, for example, and you were right, it can be very difficult to buy more at fifteen dollars, even if you think it's headed to twenty dollars. Few of us are immune to the internal debate that says, "You should have bought more at ten dollars; it's too late now to buy more."

In situations like this, though, it's important to remember an old adage of the investing business: there are only two possible investment position sizes—*way too big* or *not nearly enough*. If you use a focused scoring system for evaluating your investments, and those investments still score well, you can gain comfort that further upside exists and there's still time to buy. *Process helps separate emotion from rationality.*

The Monopoly Method uses a quantitative scoring system based on qualitative inputs. It is dynamic, meaning that an investment's "score" changes over time based on the stock price and the values assigned to eleven separate variables. The scoring is simple:

### Scoring System

1. Stocks that score from 10 to 15 are "buys."
2. Stocks that score from 8 to 10 are "holds."
3. Stocks that score below 8 require a strong reason to continue holding them or they become candidates for sale.
4. Stocks that score below 7 are considered sells, avoids, or shorting opportunities.

The process is easy, and with practice you will be able to complete a detailed picture of a potential or existing investment in less than an hour. You can perform the process on your own by visiting the Web site I have provided. Go to www.monopolymethod.com.

## The Scoring System

Scoring the variables is straightforward. You assign values from -1.0 to +1.0 (in 0.5 increments) to nine of the variables. Two of those nine—revenue growth and margin growth—receive a double weighting due to their higher significance with respect to stock price appreciation. The final two variables—catalyst and price target—receive a slightly different treatment which will be explained below. In addition, we will go through three real-world examples of using the system.

How you determine individual scores? The following will provide rough guidelines; the rest is up to you. Since this mechanism is based on subjective and qualitative inputs, the results will differ from person to person. Over time, you will get a sense of what works and what doesn't.

1. **Monopoly Factor** – Generally, a firm will not earn a full +1.0 score unless it has a dominant share of the core business it competes in. For example, Google would get a +1.0 given its high share (over 65 percent) of the online search business, and its huge lead over Microsoft and Yahoo. Companies can often merit a +0.5 if they show clear dominance in their field while still competing with many players. Companies such as Cisco Systems (CSCO), Deere (DE), Electronic Arts (ERTS), Federal Express (FDX), Fluor (FLR), Goldman Sachs (GS), Nucor (NUE), Schlumberger (SLB), and Transocean (RIG) show such dominance in their fields. The goal of the Monopoly Method is to find companies with at least a +0.5. But that's just the start: even a perfect score of +1.0 in Monopoly Method power doesn't mean a stock is an obvious buy. If its other metrics are moving in the wrong direction—particularly its revenue and margin growth—a stock will most likely underperform.

2. **Revenue Growth** – This is one of the most important considerations for a stock outperforming others. The cleanest of reported financial metrics, revenue growth—it is hard to fake revenue growth without committing outright fraud—offers a reflection of both the end market opportunity and a company's ability to differentiate itself from its peers. As a result, our process thus doubles the score associated with revenues. Look at three metrics to come to a value between -1.0 and +1.0: first is absolute growth, second is growth relative to its own history (look for acceleration), and third is growth relative to its peers.

3. **Margin Growth** – Similar to revenue growth, it's imperative to focus on margins relative to history and relative to the rest of the industry. To score a +0.5 or +1.0 on this metric, companies' margins should be higher than their peers and increasing. As with revenue growth, this variable receives double weighting in our process due to its importance to stock price movement.

4. **Financial Visibility** – Visibility relates to the likely probability of a company hitting its earnings guidance. For example, a cable company that has a base of subscribers paying monthly rates has a higher likelihood of making its projections than a company that has to move product, even if that company is Apple or General Electric. This is where data such as book-to-bill, backlog, and pipeline development comes into consideration, something I talk about extensively in the advanced knowledge section. For example, if Cisco Systems has a positive book-to-bill in a quarter (higher sales booked versus reported), then you can have more confidence in its next quarter, perhaps leading to a score of +0.5.

5. **Historical Track Record** – How well has the company done with respect to its guidance? Has it met, exceeded, or missed a portion of its estimates over the past two years? If it has met all its estimates over the past two years, it's a +1.0. If it has missed once, perhaps a +0.5. Anything worse than that is a zero at best, but more likely a negative.

6. **Balance Sheet Strength** – As discussed earlier, balance sheet structure differs by industry. The presence of debt, in other words, is not a bad thing in and of itself. A weaker balance sheet than the competition, however, is not something you're looking for, unless it's on the obvious road to improvement. Other factors to consider include inventory levels, backlog, and receivables balances.

7. **Management Quality** – How experienced is this management team? How long have they been in charge? Has the stock performed well under their tenure? Have they met their forecasts accurately? These all point to the credibility, experience, and insight management teams need to have to be successful, and more importantly, worthy of your investment dollars.

8. **Company Catalyst** – This is the only function scored from -2.0 to 2.0. Catalysts could be:

   a.  An expected financial earnings beat or miss, or
   b.  A new significant contract or client, or
   c.  An acquisition or some other significant positive or negative event, or
   d.  A significant technical point on the pricing chart.

In general, if you expect a catalyst within three months, the score is higher, as much as 2.0 if you believe it will have a big impact on the stock. Time periods of six to twelve months score roughly 1.0, and beyond that period, a zero. If you don't expect something significant to happen in the short term, the catalyst—and therefore the score—is zero. While few among us can accurately predict the future, those who occasionally do enjoy far superior investment returns than those who don't.

9. **Stock Price Target** – The best investors use a combination of upside hope and downside possibility when timing their investment decisions. In other words, what's the downside risk versus the upside reward possibility? At some point, you've got to put a number on it, even if we can all agree that predictions are rarely worth the paper they are printed on.

The formula for this metric is:

**(Price Target – Current price) / (Current Price – Downside Price)**

For example, if you believe a stock could trade from $20 to $30 over the next year, but perhaps go as low as $15, your score would be ($30 - $20)/($20 - $15) = 10/5 = 2. You should be in search of companies that give 3x to 4x type price target scores, meaning that you see the possibility of three to four times more upside than downside.

10. **Technical Strength** – The price chart of a stock tells a story that is important to factor into your investment decision. Much can be gained by focusing on the moving average, relative strength, and other indicators discussed earlier. Scoring should be based on how well a stock chart is performing relative to your chosen technical indicators. This will become more evident as we go through a few examples.

11. **Wall Street Expectations/Sentiment** – This metric measures the excitement level for a company and tries to quantify it. It is the hardest to measure in a quantitative way. *It is also a contrarian's measurement, meaning that when expectations are high, you score negative, and when they are low, you score positive.* The higher the expectations, or the more a stock runs up in anticipation of an earnings report, the lower the score—as prices move up, the return versus risk tradeoff is diminished. Sites like www.whispernumbers.com can provide some context and insight into expectations.

These eleven variables will provide extremely useful insights and will help you make better investment decisions. No method is foolproof; there will be times you are surprised by negative results and lose a portion of your investment. But the best way to avoid this risk having a significant impact on your wealth is to utilize a strong risk management approach.

### How to Construct Your Spreadsheet

There are many ways you can construct your scoring system. I have provided a template at www.monopolymethod.com, or you can create your own simple spreadsheet. The easiest method (and the one I use) is to add the components and their formulas across the columns and the individual stocks down the rows.

Please go to the Web site, where many capabilities will be available to you.

# CHAPTER SEVEN

# Putting It All Together
## Case Studies: Apple Inc., Cisco Systems, and Wal-Mart

And now, the payoff: tying it all together—philosophy, discipline, and process. This is the Monopoly Method in action.

We must strive philosophically to be in the *right place at the right time*, finding companies with wind at their backs. To review, these companies have the following characteristics:

1. High and growing market share. This should be significantly higher than the next competitor.

2. Better financial metrics than others in the industry. A higher return on capital deployed allows a company to continue to dominate and expand market share.

3. A sustained advantage that others have had difficulty replicating. Examples: Apple's iPhone, Potash's ownership of potash mining sites, and Boeing's dominance in the new airplane market. Over the long term these unfair advantages will lead to better investment returns.

We must be disciplined in gathering data to crystallize our viewpoint. The five levels of discipline are as follows:

1. Analyst Views – What do both bullish and bearish analysts think?
2. Company Information – What does the company tell you about itself?
3. Expert Networks – What do industry experts think?
4. Supply Chain Analysis – What is happening in the channel?
5. Customer – What does customer behavior tell you?

Finally, we must use a systematic, rigorous, and adjustable investment decision process. The Monopoly Method looks at eleven variables:

1. Monopoly Factor
2. Revenue Growth
3. Margin Growth
4. Financial Visibility
5. Historical Track Record
6. Balance Sheet Strength
7. Management Quality
8. Company Catalyst
9. Stock Price Target
10. Technical Strength
11. Wall Street Expectations/Sentiment

Your process must be dynamic, meaning that your scores will change with new data and price movement. If significant information is released by the company or uncovered in the marketplace, you should be prepared to change your variables at any time. Scores will change daily with stock price movement as well.

Before we get started, make sure to utilize the best research services possible. If you are an analyst at a fund, or possibly a student with professional tools, you will have superior access to information through services such as Bloomberg, First Call, Factset, Reuters, or specific brokerage firm reports. However, the advancement of the Internet has brought professional investment tools to the individual investor. A few sites worth mentioning as tools for data collection during your due diligence include (I've included many others in appendix 1):

1. Wikinvest – A great place to learn about a company.
2. Yahoo! Finance – A great place for financial estimates.
3. Money Central (an MSN Web site) – Fundamental information.
4. CNBC – Market news and company information.
5. Seeking Alpha – Investment due diligence insight.
6. Stock Charts – One of the best charting sites available.

## Case Study #1 Apple Inc. (AAPL) – August 2010

### Philosophy:
### What Is the Theme?
### Where Do They Have Potential to Dominate?
### What Is the Potential Investment Opportunity?

**Thematic Forces:** Apple is exposed to multiple billion-dollar markets, which are growing significantly. The company is well positioned in the following themes: growth of consumer digital lifestyles, including music, video, and computing; growth in mobile applications, including voice, data, and multimedia for both the consumer and the business user; and lastly, the development of the Internet as a medium of communication, content delivery, and consumer and business commerce.

**Business Description:** Apple designs, manufactures, and markets personal computers, mobile communication devices, and portable digital music and video players, as well as sells related software, services, peripherals, and networking solutions. The company, formerly known as Apple Computer, Inc., was founded in 1976 and is headquartered in Cupertino, California.

## Figure 7.1 Apple Price Chart

Source: www.stockcharts.com

## The 11 Variables of Investment Selection:

**Monopoly Factor:** There are few people today who wouldn't consider Apple a very strong and powerful company. However, the nature of its market presence is often misunderstood. For all its brand recognition, Apple commands a very low percentage of overall global consumer computer sales. What's more, its percentage of sales within corporations is even lower. On the other hand, it utterly dominates the music player business (iPod), is the hands-down winner thus far in the smartphone market (iPhone), and almost single-handedly put the netbook (small, inexpensive, lightweight, Internet-only computers) market on the ropes with the iPad. Apple can certainly be viewed as having monopolistic tendencies. More to the point, given its very high market share in multiple billion-dollar markets, the stock deserves the highest rating, +1.0.

**Revenue Growth:** While the past few years have been difficult for most technology and electronics suppliers, Apple has grown significantly. Looking back eight quarters, we can see clearly, on a year-over-year (YOY) basis, that Apple's revenue growth has actually accelerated, from +36 percent in its June 2008 quarter to +49 percent in March 2010:

### Year-over-year Revenue Trends

| Q3 2008 (June): +36% | Q3 2009: +29% |
|---|---|
| Q4 2008: +74% | Q4 2009: +6% |
| Q1 2009: +14% | Q1 2010: +32% |
| Q2 2009: +14% | Q2 2010: +49% |

Apple's growth slowed meaningfully in 2009 due to the global recession. Thus, the accelerating growth we are seeing now is partially a result of comparing to very weak numbers. To get a better sense of the "normalized" growth—growth that we would see in a normal business environment—we should look at growth estimates for the current year, which are above 15 percent. That's worth a +0.5 on our rating scale. However, the release of the iPad in April 2010, which at the time of this writing has sold over three million units in the first ninety days, seems to be setting Apple up for possibly higher growth than that 15 percent. I believe it deserves the highest rating, a +1.0.

Now, let's look at it from a sequential point of view. It is important to realize that almost all companies have some sort of seasonality associated with their business. Apple is no exception—its first quarter, which ends in December—is always the best, due to holiday sales. Its fourth quarter also tends to be strong, due to the back-to-school season. The two middle quarters tend to be weaker.

**Sequential Revenue Trends**

| Q3 2008 (June): -5% | Q3 2009: +7% |
|---|---|
| Q4 2008: +52% | Q4 2009: +25% |
| Q1 2009: +3% | Q1 2010: +28% |
| Q2 2009: -24% | Q2 2010: -14% |

What we see here is improvement. The sequential growth from Q4 2009 of +25 percent to Q1 of 2010 of +28 percent was much better than the previous year's +3 percent shift. One has to take into account that 2009 was a recession year, but the sequential momentum is intact and supports the strong score we've given.

**Margin Growth:** Computer costs do not change much on a seasonal basis, so an analysis of costs can focus on sequential results. While any margin expansion is good news, gross margin expansion is preferable to operating margin expansion.

**Sequential Gross Margin Trends**

| Q3 2008 (June): 36% | Q3 2009: 40.9% |
|---|---|
| Q4 2008: 39% | Q4 2009: 41.8% |
| Q1 2009: 37.9% | Q1 2010: 40.9% |
| Q2 2009: 39.9% | Q2 2010: 41.7% |

You can see the true dominance of this company by its consistent and strong margin performance—margins have increased during an incredibly difficult business period. Margin growth has slowed, but is still positive, so unless we see acceleration again, a score of +0.5 is appropriate. Newer products, such as the iPhone and iPad, carry higher margins than the traditional desktop or notebook computer products. This should have a positive effect on future margins.

**Financial Visibility:** Because most technology companies ship products soon after you order them, there is very little backlog, which is products that have been ordered but not yet shipped. As a result, despite optimism about the company's prospects, it is always difficult to forecast future results. We certainly can't say Apple has the same visibility of a telephone company, which generally knows its revenues a few quarters in advance. As a result, a +0.5 is warranted for this criterion.

**Historical Track Record:** Track record is a challenging metric to score because it relies on experience. It is also a very important metric since it relates to management's ability to understand and forecast its business. This is clearly critical if you are going to hand over your hard-earned money. The track record component measures the management team's ability to meet their goals or the guidance they have given to Wall Street. The good news about a company's track record is that the longer you know a company, the better your ability to score will be. In Apple's case, I would have to give it a +1.0, as it has a history of being conservative and generally correct in its guidance.

**Balance Sheet Strength:** This is a balance sheet score, and represents the overall financial health of the company. In many cases in the technology sector—where very little debt and leverage is deployed—all companies score +1.0. Certainly, this is the case with Apple, which has over $30 billion in cash and short-term investments.

**Management Quality:** You might say that this is similar to the track record, as a high-quality management team will be one that accurately forecasts its business. However, there are other factors as well to a high-quality management team. Those factors include:

1. Length of time with the company
2. Ability to create value through acquisitions
3. Experience during both good times and bad times

In Apple's case, Steve Jobs is a legendary figure who became CEO in the early 1990s, has withstood the test of time, and has managed through many different environments. In addition, he has pushed Apple into many successful businesses, such as the phone and tablet markets. For this reason, Apple scores a +1.0.

**Company Catalyst:** Many investors utilize this method as their main investment trigger, attempting to forecast specific single events, such as earnings, acquisitions, or new product announcements. Within the Monopoly Method, it is only one component, but with a scoring ability up to 2.0, it is an important one. In Apple's case, there isn't anything significant that we are expecting (since it already announced and is shipping the iPad), so the score becomes a zero. (One might argue that the iPad will be more or less successful than people are expecting and score this factor differently.)

**Stock Price Target:** Every investment should have an upside and downside price. There are many ways to come up with a price target that makes sense—either on your own, with the use of other investors' numbers, or researching many Web sites and Wall Street analysts that make their price targets available.

In Apple's case, the current stock is about $250, and since we are looking at a twelve-month price target, it is reasonable to look into 2011 earnings estimates and work backward. In addition, since Apple is a technology stock, and growth is at the core of our analysis, earnings and P/E ratios are an appropriate tool. Let's look at the process.

What is the possible upside price of Apple in one year, the fall of 2011? Since stocks discount the future, in September 2011, Apple should be trading based on its September fiscal year end 2012 estimates of over $18 a share. Apple has generally traded with an average P/E over 20x, something you can easily calculate by going back through its earnings and prices. On this metric alone, a year from now Apple should be trading at 20 x $18, or $360. *(At the time of publication in the summer of 2011, the stock was over $350, vastly exceeding earnings estimates, leading to changes in the metrics and still showing a buy rating!)*

In some cases, finding estimates for future years may prove difficult to an individual investor. In these cases, look at the farthest out estimate and gauge your price target on this. As an example, on the CNBC site, the best projection is for earnings in fiscal year 2011 of $15.71. Applying a P/E multiple of 20x provides a very conservative estimate, since stocks tend to trade on future, not current earnings—which will be the case a year from now. That gives you $315, for a minimum return of 26 percent.

Another strategy would be to increase the earnings by a similar amount in FY 2012 as compared to the $15.71 estimate for FY 2011. In this case, $15.71 + 15% = $18, and we are back to our $360 target. The beauty of this system is its ability to be flexible. You can enter $315 or $360 as your target and see how it affects your results. In fact, you may find that in order to justify an investment in Apple you need a certain price target. Knowing what your price target has to be to make an investment viable is a very important characteristic of a successful investor.

On the downside, while we can look to periods of weakness in the markets as a barometer, a better strategy is to use technical analysis and look at moving averages. The 50-day moving average is the first level of risk management, which in this case is at or about the level of the current stock price. The 200-day moving average is the level, if broken, at which one should consider reviewing his or her investment thesis. Apple's 200-day moving average is $212 and is a good estimate of downside risk. Should Apple trend down toward this level, it would represent an area to be buying the stock, but should it break this level and remain below for a week or so, the positive case for Apple is in jeopardy.

So the Risk/Return formula is (using a target between $315 and $360):

**Upside (Future Price – Current Price) / Downside (Current Price – Downside)**

($337.50 - $250) / ($250 - $212) = 2.3

With a downside price target at $212, the score becomes 2.3, meaning you have 2.3x as much upside, or $87.50, compared to the downside of $38. By utilizing this approach and timing your investments when they have the greatest scores, you will increase your chances for a successful return. For example, if the market fell and carried Apple with it to a price of $230, your upside/downside would now be $107.50/$18 for a score of almost 6.0. This is the power of this system; it helps you invest at the right time.

## Technical Strength:

*Moving Average (MA)*

As you can see in figure 7.1, Apple is trading above its 50-day moving average and above its 200-day moving average. This fact alone would generally be considered positive, but a few more observations can be drawn:

A. The 50-day MA has not been a particularly good indicator, since it has been broken a few times recently. The 200-day is far better support, which also coincides with the downside price target used above.

B. Both the 50-day and 200-day MA are on an upward slope, meaning the trend remains upwardly biased.

*Relative Strength (RSI)*

Relative strength (RSI) is an indicator that measures the rate at which a stock is moving up or down (i.e., its momentum). When a stock moves up or down rapidly, it could be considered overbought or oversold, and the probability of making a profitable trade in the trend direction is lower. Readings above 70 are considered overbought and readings below 30 are considered oversold.

Apple is trading at a neutral RSI reading of about 50. Given the favorable technical bias we see with the two indicators above, we can conclude that a score of 0.5 is appropriate. It should be noted that there are other technical indicators one can use to form an opinion, and we will talk about a few of them in the advanced knowledge section.

**Wall Street Expectations/Sentiment:** Everything on Wall Street revolves around expectations, both at the level of individual stocks and for the market as a whole. We are constantly "expecting" something to happen. It follows, then, that when making an investment, whether it is on the long side, short side, long-term, or just a quick trade, one has to be aware of what is "expected" from one's holdings. Of course, there is no "expectations" metric or indicator, so one has to infer this information from conducting due diligence and judge for oneself if expectations are high or low. In addition, expectations are always reset after each quarter, so that when you make an investment or contemplate one, take your time frame into account.

Even though there are no hard metrics, there are a few (technical and fundamental) ways we can go about making that inference, thereby providing us a way to score the stock, including:

1. Where is a stock trading relative to its historic P/E ratio?
2. Where is a stock trading technically? Is it in overbought or oversold territory?
3. How much do we hear about the stock in the press, either in print or on television and the Web?
4. Has the stock been recently upgraded or downgraded by multiple brokerage firms?

Currently, Apple is trading below its historic P/E levels of over 20x on current year estimates. From the technical section, we can infer that it is in slightly positive territory, being neither extremely overbought nor oversold. With a new product cycle unfolding (iPad), a launch of a new phone (iPhone 4), increasing margins, and a recovering economy, we could make the case that Apple should trade at a premium to its historical P/E multiple. This suggests that expectations are generally too low. On this basis alone, a score of +1.0 is likely justified, but one only has to look at the price chart to see that Apple's stock has performed admirably over the past year, so it's hard to say that it's undervalued. For this reason, I am going to be conservative and score it +0.5, as opposed to +1.0.

## Putting It All Together

### Scoring Methodology

- A score greater than 10 and less than 15 is considered a strong buy. It is possible to get scores greater than 15, especially as a stock gets close to its downside price target, but be careful of a score this high when you are conducting your due diligence. Stocks are often cheap for a good reason.

- A score from 8 to 10 is considered a hold, meaning that there is likely upside over time, but it is close to being fairly valued.
- A score from 5 to 8 is overvalued and could be a candidate for a short sale.
- A score below 5 is generally a sale, avoid, or short.

## Score

| Monopoly Method Score | 10.8 |
|---|---|
| Monopoly Factor | 1.0 |
| Revenue Growth | 1.0 |
| Margin Growth | 0.5 |
| Financial Visibility | 0.5 |
| Historical Track Record | 1.0 |
| Balance Sheet Strength | 1.0 |
| Management Quality | 1.0 |
| Company Catalyst | 0.0 |
| Stock Price Target | 2.3 |
| Technical Strength | 0.5 |
| Expectations/Sentiment | 0.5 |
| Total | 10.8 |

Apple, at $250 per share, is a BUY. It is likely undervalued and should be bought or over-weighted in your portfolio at these levels. If Apple's price moves up to $260, the score goes down into the "high end" of the hold area, meaning one should not add to the position unless a revised price target is formulated. It is important to understand that the earnings and scores can and likely will change from quarter to quarter.

**Note:** *At the time of publication in the summer of 2011, Apple had exceeded estimates significantly and many of the metrics would have been adjusted along the way. Most impressive is the change in earnings estimates for FY 2011 (September 2011) from the $15.71 we used in the example to the current estimate of almost $23 per share. Had you utilized the Monopoly Method process in the fall of 2010, given it was rated a buy, the stock would have been a strong candidate for your portfolio. As the company exceeded the estimates, your price target would have moved up, keeping the stock at a buy rating. For example, based on current estimates, a price target of 20x P/E = $460 is reasonable, making it still attractive. Go to www.monopolymethod.com and score it again!*

## Case Study #2 Cisco Systems (CSCO) – Fall 2010

### <u>Philosophy:</u>
### What Is the Theme?
### Where Do They Have Potential to Dominate?
### What Is the Potential Investment Opportunity?

**Thematic Forces:** While the telecommunications industry is mature overall, Cisco is positioned well in the following themes: growth of consumer digital life-styles, next-generation Internet infrastructure, and the increasing use of the Internet for mobile voice, data, and video usage.

**Business Description:** Cisco Systems supplies voice, data, and video networking equipment and services to consumers, businesses, and service providers globally.

### Figure 7.2 Cisco Price Chart

Source: www.stockcharts.com

## The 11 Variables of Investment Selection:

**Monopoly Factor:** Cisco Systems has long had a dominant role in communication networks globally. Cisco went public in 1990 with about $69 million in sales, and today's sales are over $36 billion. During this twenty-year period, Cisco has managed to outgrow its peers and retain higher margins while also remaining active in the acquisition markets, especially during difficult economic periods. While it dominates many segments, it would be hard to describe it as a monopoly; rather, it has strong monopolistic tendencies. We can't score a +1.0, as its market share is not high enough, but a +0.5 seems very reasonable.

**Revenue Growth:** In the past few years, both Cisco and the broader industry have seen growth slow, especially since the onset of the financial crisis in November 2007. On a year-over-year basis, the firm saw revenue growth fall from +10 percent in April 2008 to negative 13 percent in October 2009, with an increasingly negative trend. However, we also see the seeds of a recovery starting in Cisco's Q2 2010, which ended in January 2010:

### Year-over-year Revenue Trends

| | |
|---|---|
| Q3 2008 (April): +10% | Q3 2009: -17% |
| Q4 2008: +10% | Q4 2009: -18% |
| Q1 2009: +8% | Q1 2010: -13% |
| Q2 2009: -8% | Q2 2010: +8% |

Now, let's look at it from a sequential point of view. Remember, it is important to realize almost all companies have some sort of seasonality associated with their business, the most frequent being a strong Q4 followed by a weak Q1.

### Sequential Revenue Trends

| | |
|---|---|
| Q3 2008 (April): +0% | Q3 2009: -10% |
| Q4 2008 (July): +6% | Q4 2009: +5% |
| Q1 2009: +0% | Q1 2010: +2% |
| Q2 2009: -12% | Q2 2010: +2% |

The insight gained here is that revenues growth started to reverse in Q3 2009, a full two quarters before the change shows up in the year-over-year data above. The stock bottomed around this time as well.

We can conclude from this analysis that revenue growth has bottomed for now and is recovering. A cautious perspective: that revenues will indeed rebound, but it's too soon to predict a strong and enduring rebound. Score: +0.5.

**Margin Growth:** Similar to the revenue factor, to derive our views on Cisco's profitability, look both backward for two years and forward for a few quarters. Since costs do not change significantly on a seasonal basis, we can focus our work on sequential data. Remember, while any margin expansion is good news, gross margin expansion is preferable to operating margin expansion.

**Sequential Gross Margin Trends**

| Period | GM | Period | GM | Period | GM |
|--------|-----|---------|-------|---------|-------|
| Q1 2008 | 66% | Q1 2009 | 65.6% | Q1 2010 | 64.5% |
| Q2 2008 | 66% | Q2 2009 | 64% | Q2 2010 | 64.7% |
| Q3 2008 | 66% | Q3 2009 | 65.1% | | |
| Q4 2008 | 65% | Q4 2009 | 65.3% | | |

Immediately you can see the true dominance of this company by its consistent and strong margin performance. During one of the most challenging economic periods since the Great Depression, Cisco was able hold its margins relatively steady. While we can't point to significant margin growth, we can position that margins likely bottomed in Q2 2009 (January 2009) and have trended positive since then. Similar to revenues, the direction is right, but the momentum is a bit weak. This warrants a +0.5 rating.

**Financial Visibility:** At first glance, one could look at Cisco's technology roots and consider that financial visibility is challenging. However, given Cisco's dominance, it has a better record than most others in its peer group. A common way to determine a visibility score is to review the past earnings conference calls for comments on the company's "book-to-bill." The "book-to-bill" gives you a measure of the strength of its forward momentum (and last quarter it was above 1.0), since it measures how many sales were booked versus product shipped in a given quarter. A book-to-bill greater than 1.0 is a good sign and less than 1.0 a troubling sign. In Cisco's case, since it is coming out of a recession and is generally conservative, we can score it a +1.0.

**Historical Track Record:** This is a challenging metric to score because it relies on experience. However, it is a very important metric since it relates to management's ability to understand and forecast its business. Track record should be a measure of the management team's ability to meet their goals or the guidance they have given to Wall Street. One only has to look at their past press releases or listen to a few conference calls to understand that Cisco earns a +1.0, as historically they have been conservative and generally correct in their guidance.

**Balance Sheet Strength:** This balance sheet score, as you recall, represents the overall financial health of the company. In many cases, especially within the technology sector where very little debt and leverage is deployed, all companies score +1.0. Certainly, this is the case with Cisco, which has over $30 billion in cash and short-term investments. There are many companies that deploy leverage (debt) or otherwise have issues with working capital, so make sure you look at the appropriate ratios.

**Management Quality:** Once again, a high-quality management team is one that accurately forecasts its business, in addition to many other factors, such as:

1. Length of time with the company
2. Ability to create value through acquisitions
3. Experience during both good times and bad times

In Cisco's case, John Chambers, who became CEO in the early 1990s, has withstood the test of time and has managed through many different environments. In addition, he has pushed Cisco into many successful businesses. For this reason, Cisco scores a +1.0.

**Company Catalyst:** Many investors utilize this method as their main investment style, attempting to forecast specific single point events, such as earnings, acquisitions, and new products. In Cisco's case, there isn't anything significant on the horizon, so the score is a zero.

**Stock Price Target:** In Cisco's case, the current stock in June 2010 is about $23, and since we are looking at a twelve-month price target, it is reasonable to look into 2011 earnings estimates and work backward. In addition, since Cisco is a technology stock and growth is at the core of our analysis, earnings and P/E ratios are appropriate tools. (More detail on the specific variables that are important to each sector can be found by looking at Chapter Three.) Let's look at the process one more time in detail:

1. What will the price of Cisco be in one year = Fall 2011?

2. Since stocks discount the future, in September 2011, Cisco should be trading based on its July fiscal year end 2012. Cisco has generally traded with an average P/E over 18x, something you can easily calculate by going back through the earnings and prices. On the CNBC Web site the best projection is for earnings in Fiscal Year 2011 of $1.59. At a P/E multiple of 18x, a very conservative estimate, since stocks tend to trade on future, not current earnings (which will be the case a year from now), the price would be about $29, for a minimum return of 26 percent. Another strategy would be to increase the

earnings by a similar amount in FY 2012, as compared to the $1.59 estimate for FY 2011. In this case, in FY 2011, the estimates are for growth of 14 percent over FY 2010 (EPS of $1.59 versus $1.39), so 14 percent growth on top of $1.59 is $1.81. If we then multiply by the average P/E of 18x we get a price target of $32.50, for a potential gain of over 40 percent. *Remember, knowing what your price target has to be to make an investment viable is a very important characteristic of a successful investor, and to be able to accomplish this throughout your portfolio will lead to better stock selection and stronger profits.*

3.  Once again, on the downside, while we can look to periods of weakness in the markets as a barometer, a better strategy is to look technically at moving averages, which often give insight into the future. The 50-day moving average is the first level of risk management, which in this case is above the current price at approximately $23.50—a troubling sign. The 50-day is considered more of a short-term support level and, if broken, is a warning sign, but generally not considered significant. The 200-day moving average is the level at which, if broken, one should consider reviewing one's investment thesis. Cisco's 200-day moving average is $24.32, and again, the stock is below this level. Remember from our prior example with Apple, the 200-day moving average is a good estimate of downside risk, and should Cisco trend down toward this level, it would represent an area to be buying the stock, but since it has broken this level over an extended period, the positive case for Cisco is in jeopardy. This knowledge alone might persuade an investor to hold off on a potential investment. Our next level of support is between $18 and $20, a level it reached in 2009. For the purposes of this analysis, this would be the appropriate level to use.

4.  In this case, the formula is (using the midpoint of the targets):

Upside (Future Price – Current Price) / Downside (Current Price – Downside)

$$(\$30.50 - \$22.50) / (\$22.50 - \$19.00) = \$8/\$3.5 = 2.3$$

With our downside price target at $19, the score becomes 2.3, meaning we have 2.3x as much upside ($8.00) compared to our downside ($3.50).

**Technical Strength:** We've already done some work on this variable, since we used technical analysis to measure our downside. We will add Relative Strength as well.

1.  Moving Average (50-day, 200-day)
2.  Relative Strength

*Moving Average (MA)*

As you can see from the price chart, Cisco is trading below its 50-day moving average and below its 200-day moving average. This fact alone would generally be considered negative, but a few more observations can be drawn:

A. The 50-day MA is broken and the curve has turned downward, a negative sign.

B. The 200-day MA, though, is still on an upward-sloping curve (just barely), which could be considered a slight positive.

*Relative Strength (RSI)*

Relative strength (RSI) is an indicator that measures the rate at which a stock is moving up or down (i.e., its momentum). When a stock moves up or down rapidly, it could be considered overbought or oversold, and the probability of making a profitable trade in the trend direction is lower. Readings above 70 are considered overbought and readings below 30 are considered oversold.

In this case, we see Cisco is trading at a very oversold level, an RSI reading of about 29. The technicals for Cisco are not very good and a negative score is warranted. In this case, since the RSI is extremely oversold and the 200-day still has a slight positive bias to it, a score of -0.5 should be sufficient.

**Wall Street Expectations/Sentiment:** Since we know everything on Wall Street revolves around expectations, what can we tell about Cisco? To remind you, even though there are no hard metrics, there are a few ways we can go about scoring a stock's expectations, including:

1. Where is a stock trading relative to its historic P/E ratio?
2. Where is a stock trading technically, being either in overbought or oversold territory?
3. How much do we hear about the stock in the press, either in print or on television and the Web?
4. Has the stock been recently upgraded or downgraded by multiple brokerage firms?

Cisco is trading below its historic P/E levels of about 18x on current year estimates, and from the technical section, we can infer that it is in neutral to oversold territory. In addition, we have not heard significant noise in the press or from Wall Street analysts regarding the company. (Look for press releases or other newsworthy information.) All of this suggests that expectations are generally in line, but the stock is trading at oversold levels and below its historical valuation. A score of +0.5 is appropriate.

## Putting It All Together

### Scoring Methodology

- A score greater than 10 and less than 15 is considered a strong buy. It is possible to get scores greater than 15, especially as a stock gets close to its downside price target, but be careful of a score this high when you are conducting your due diligence. Stocks are often cheap for a good reason.
- A score from 8 to 10 is considered a hold, meaning that there is likely upside over time, but it is close to being fairly valued.
- A score from 5 to 8 is overvalued and could be a candidate for a short sale.
- A score below 5 is generally a sale, avoid, or short.

### Score

| Monopoly Method Score | 8.8 |
|---|---|
| Monopoly Factor | 0.5 |
| Revenue Growth | 0.5 |
| Margin Growth | 0.5 |
| Financial Visibility | 1.0 |
| Historical Track Record | 1.0 |
| Balance Sheet Strength | 1.0 |
| Management Quality | 1.0 |
| Company Catalyst | 0.0 |
| Stock Price Target | 2.3 |
| Technical Strength | -0.5 |
| Expectations/Sentiment | 0.5 |
| **Total** | **8.8** |

From the score above we see that Cisco, at $21.30 per share, is in the middle of a hold, meaning that it is likely fairly valued to undervalued. At this price, assuming earnings can grow at 15 percent, your gains should at least equal this level and, according to your portfolio position sizing comfort level, an "average" position is warranted. To become more bullish (meaning that you would overweight Cisco in your portfolio), you would have to expect Cisco's financial earnings performance to be ahead of Wall Street expectations or the price would have to move down with no accompanying negative news. If Cisco's price fell to $20, it would be time to overweight the stock.

**Note:** *At the time of publication in the summer of 2011, Cisco had missed two quarters in a row, and was trading around the $20 level. Had you utilized the Monopoly Method process in the fall of 2010, given it was rated a hold, your position sizing would have been smaller, and you would have been in a better position to add, if it was still attractive. Note, though, that since the company has missed two quarters in a row, some of the scores (revenue growth, margins, track record, financial visibility, risk/return price objective) could and should be negatively changed to reflect the current environment. Go to www.monopolymethod.com and score it again!*

## Case Study #3 Wal-Mart (WMT)

### <u>Philosophy:</u>
**What Is the Theme?**
**Where Do They Have Potential to Dominate?**
**What Is the Potential Investment Opportunity?**

**Thematic Forces:** Wal-Mart is the largest employer in the United States and continues to grow by focusing on entering different categories of products domestically, but the real engine of growth is taking its systems and approach to international markets.

**Business Description:** Wal-Mart Stores, Inc., operates retail stores in various formats on a global basis. As of January 31, 2010, it operated 803 discount stores, 2,747 supercenters, 158 neighborhood markets, and 596 Sam's Clubs in the United States. International units are: Argentina (43), Brazil (434), Canada (317), Chile (252), Costa Rica (170), El Salvador (77), Guatemala (164), Honduras (53), India (1), Japan (371), Mexico (1,469), Nicaragua (55), Puerto Rico (56), the United Kingdom (371), as well as the People's Republic of China (279). The company was founded in 1945 and is based in Bentonville, Arkansas.

### <u>Figure 7.3 Wal-Mart Price Chart</u>

Source: www.stockcharts.com

## The 11 Variables of Investment Selection:

**Monopoly Factor:** I don't think anyone would question Wal-Mart's domination in the U.S., and increasingly it is being perceived in this light globally. One of the key attributes of a monopoly is "pricing power," which Wal-Mart has and uses to its advantage. For this reason the company merits the highest score of 1.0.

## Revenue Growth:

### Year-over-year Revenue Trends

| | |
|---|---|
| Q2 Fiscal 2009 (July): +10% | Q2 2010: -1% |
| Q3 2009: +7% | Q3 2010: +1% |
| Q4 2009: +1% | Q4 2010 (ends Jan 2010): +5% |
| Q1 2010: -1% | Q1 2011: +6% |

On a year-over-year basis, we can see that growth is accelerating, coming off a period of flat growth.

### Sequential Revenue Trends

| | |
|---|---|
| Q2 Fiscal 2009 (July): +8% | Q2 2010: +7% |
| Q3 2009: -4% | Q3 2010: -1% |
| Q4 2009: +11% | Q4 2010 (ends Jan 2010): +14% |
| Q1 2010: -13% | Q1 2011: -12% |

On the surface, it is hard to make any real conclusion from the above numbers. On a deeper level, though, there are positive signs. Wal-Mart is a retailer, thus seasonality is a big issue, making consistent sequential growth difficult. (Generally, only retailers in their early years will grow each quarter, since they are adding stores on an accelerated basis.) However, if we look at year-over-year sequential trends, meaning how Wal-Mart did, for example, sequentially in its Q4 2010 versus Q4 2009 on a sequential basis we see a trend. In Q4 2010 (January 2010), its sales posted a sequential rise of 14 percent versus 11 percent in the prior year, while revenues in the following quarter were down less sequentially than in the previous year. This is an indication of renewed growth.

We can conclude from this analysis that revenue growth has bottomed for now and is recovering. Score: +0.5.

**Margin Growth:** Remember, while any margin expansion is good news, gross margin expansion is preferable to operating margin expansion.

**Sequential Gross Margin Trends**

| Period | Gross Margin | Period | Gross Margin |
|--------|--------------|--------|--------------|
| Q2 2009 | 23.6% | Q2 2010 | 24.9% |
| Q3 2009 | 24.1% | Q3 2010 | 25.2% |
| Q4 2009 | 23.5% | Q4 2010 | 24.4% |
| Q1 2010 | 24.7% | Q1 2011 | 24.6% |

It is easy to see the dominance of this company by its consistent and strong margin performance. For a retailer, margins in this range are considered especially strong. During the challenging times of 2008 and 2009, Wal-Mart was able to hold on to its margins. However, while margins are stable, growth is not evident, thus a score of zero is appropriate.

**Financial Visibility:** Given that Wal-Mart is the largest employer in the United States, the company's financial visibility is connected to the overall economy in the U.S. and overseas. This presents both positive and negative implications. Since it is so large, moving the needle is a bit harder, thus forecasting is easier. On the negative side, forecasting the momentum of the economy is a challenging job for even the most experienced investor. Since we know that Wal-Mart is a retailer, glancing at the advanced knowledge section at the end of the book tells us we can also look at other metrics, such as trends in monthly sales and new store openings, to give us visibility. Given its size, its ability to forecast is generally strong, earning it a score of +0.5.

**Historical Track Record:** By looking back through former earnings releases and listening to a few conference calls, one can see that, while not perfect, Wal-Mart has a good long-term track record of meeting Wall Street estimates—not too hot, and not too cold. Another +0.5.

**Balance Sheet Strength:** There is no question Wal-Mart deserves the highest rating here. A +1.0 it is.

**Management Quality:** Wal-Mart has always had top-tier management within its organization and it is one of the few companies to have grown so rapidly over many years. The only negative one could point out—over the past *five* years, growth has slowed considerably. A new CEO was appointed in 2009, and although he had been there since 2005, his ability to manage Wal-Mart is untested. Due to these factors, another +0.5 is merited.

**Company Catalyst:** In Wal-Mart's case, there isn't anything significant that we are expecting, so the score is a zero.

**Stock Price Target:** In Wal-Mart's case, the current stock in June 2010 is about $50, and since we are looking at a twelve-month price target, it is reasonable to look into 2011 earnings estimates and work backward. In addition, since Wal-Mart is a retail stock, growth again is at the core of our analysis, and earnings and P/E ratios are an appropriate tool. (More detail on the specific variables that are important to each sector can be found by looking at Chapter Three.)

A.   What will the price of Wal-Mart be in one year = Fall 2011?

B.   In September 2011, Wal-Mart should be trading based on its January fiscal year ending 2012. (Since it is only a month into 2011, really this is more akin to 2011 earnings.) Wal-Mart has generally traded with an average P/E of about 12x to 13x, something you can easily calculate by going back through the earnings and prices, or by looking at Yahoo Finance or wikinvest. On the Yahoo Finance Web site the best projection is for earnings in Fiscal Year 2012 of $4.39. At a P/E multiple of 13x, a very conservative estimate, since stocks tend to trade on future, not current earnings (which will be the case a year from now), the price would be about $57, for a minimum return of 14 percent.

C.   Since Wal-Mart is trading below all its moving averages, let's look at where support may be. It's clear from chart 7.3 that around $46, Wal-Mart has strong support. This should be used as our downside.

D.   In this case, the formula is (using the midpoint of the targets):

Upside (Future Price – Current Price) / Downside (Current Price – Downside)

$$(\$57 - \$50) / (\$50 - \$46) = \$7/\$4 = 1.75$$

With our downside price target at $46, the score becomes 1.75, meaning we have 1.75x as much upside ($7.00) compared to our downside ($4.00).

**Technical Strength:** We've already done some work on this variable, since we used technical analysis to measure our downside. We will add Relative Strength as well.

1.   Moving Average (50-day, 200-day)
2.   Relative Strength

*Moving Average (MA)*

As you can see from the price chart, Wal-Mart is trading below its 50-day moving average and below its 200-day moving average. This fact alone would generally be considered negative, but a few more observations can be drawn:

A.  The 50-day MA is broken and the curve has turned downward, a negative sign.

B.  The 200-day MA, though, is still on an upward-sloping curve (just barely), which could be considered a slight positive.

*Relative Strength (RSI)*

Readings above 70 are considered overbought and readings below 30 are considered oversold. In this case, we see Wal-Mart is trading in the middle, with an RSI reading of about 46. The technicals for Wal-Mart are not very good and a negative score is warranted. Since the 200-day still has a slight positive bias to it, a score of -0.5 should be sufficient.

**Wall Street Expectations/Sentiment:** Wal-Mart is trading at roughly its historic P/E levels of about 12x to 13x on next year's estimates, and from the technical section, we can infer that it is in neutral territory. All of this suggests that expectations are generally in line, so a score of zero is appropriate.

## Putting It All Together

## Scoring Methodology

*   Scores greater than 10 and less than 15 is considered a buy. It is possible to get scores greater than 15, especially as a stock gets close to its downside price target, but be careful of a score this high.
*   Scores from 8 to 10 are considered holds, meaning that there is likely upside over time, but it is close to being fairly valued.
*   Scores from 5 to 8 suggest a stock is overvalued and could be a candidate for a sale or short sale.
*   Scores below 5 indicates a sale, avoid, or short sale.

## Score

| Monopoly Method Score | 5.75 |
|---|---|
| Monopoly Factor | 1.0 |
| Revenue Growth | 0.5 |
| Margin Growth | 0.0 |
| Financial Visibility | 0.5 |
| Historical Track Record | 0.5 |
| | |
| Balance Sheet Strength | 1.0 |
| Management Quality | 0.5 |
| Company Catalyst | 0.0 |
| Stock Price Target | 1.75 |
| Technical Strength | -0.5 |
| Expectations/Sentiment | 0.0 |
| **Total** | **5.75** |

From the score above we see that Wal-Mart, at $50 per share, is not attractive despite its monopoly power. For it to become attractive, the price would have to decrease below $48, at which level the score would increase to over 8. But at current prices, a position in Wal-Mart is not merited until it moves lower or your price target moves higher.

**Note:** *At the time of publication in the summer of 2011, Wal-Mart was victim to two poor quarters in a row, and was trading around the $53 level, up a very small amount over the past six months. Had you utilized the Monopoly Method process in the fall of 2010, given it was rated a sell or avoid, you would have missed out on a very small gain. However, had you utilized this capital and deployed it toward a buy rated stock, such as Apple, your return would have been far higher. Similar to Cisco, since the company has missed two quarters in a row, some of the scores (revenue growth, margins, track record, financial visibility, risk/return price objective) could and should be negatively changed to reflect the current environment. Go to www.monopolymethod.com and score it again!*

# CHAPTER EIGHT

# Portfolio and Risk Management
## How to Manage Your Whole Portfolio

We approach managing our *whole* portfolio in much the same way we approach each stock, with philosophy, discipline, and process.

Portfolio and risk management go hand in hand, as one relates to the other. As an investor, whether you are an individual or part of a larger organization, the management of the portfolio should be an active process similar to the process of selecting one's investments.

**Philosophy:** Portfolio management strategy should remain consistent and rarely change. Of course, there will be times when you will need to adjust your strategy (more conservative or risky), given a particular change in the overall market dynamics or other factors. Portfolio strategy should also encompass risk management.

**Discipline:** Discipline is what separates the best managers and investors from the rest of the pack. Once you find the right combination of individual investment selection and portfolio strategy, stick by it, learn from it, and only adjust if you have the data to support it. Remember, by being disciplined, you can create a strategy that is repeatable, scalable, and allows you to measure the results. With measurement you are not reacting blindly, but are adjusting intelligently.

**Process:** If you create a consistent process to managing your portfolio, each investment opportunity will fit appropriately. For example, if you determine that equities should represent 50 percent of your asset allocation, then when you achieve this level any new position should only be added if one is removed. Utilizing an approach such as the Monopoly Method process can help prioritize your investments based on risk and return.

## Philosophy

A portfolio philosophy should always start with an analysis of your overall investment objectives. It is beyond the scope of this book to provide specific strategies for each type of investor, but we can speak to the main factors that every portfolio should consider.

**Diversification:** A portfolio by definition is a collection of investments meant to provide diversification. The goal of diversification is to minimize risk. For example, in the 1990s when the technology bubble burst, many investors who thought they were diversified because they held many stocks were hit very hard since most of their stocks were in one sector, technology. If you are an individual, it is crucial to diversify across many investment types, including bonds, stocks, commodities, and hard assets such as real estate. Just as important, there must be some level of diversification within each asset class as well. So, within equities, make sure you have exposure to multiple sectors if possible, such as financials, technology, industrials, and consumer goods companies. As a whole, a portfolio is constructed in order to minimize the risk of one bad investment having too big of an impact. There are many views as to the number of investments it takes to be diversified, while still having few enough to benefit from the success of a single holding. I recommend building a portfolio of fifteen to twenty stocks across multiple sectors.

**Risk Management:** This idea should be self-explanatory, and in many cases depends on your personal circumstances. However, many investors don't realize or understand how much risk is incorporated in their portfolios. There are three primary ways an investor can look at total risk.

A. **Beta:** Portfolio beta is the easiest to understand. Beta is defined as the historical change in the value of a security relative to the market as a whole. To view your portfolio beta, simply multiply the beta of each investment by its percentage weighting in your portfolio, then add these together. This will give you a measure of your risk relative to the market. Beta gives you an understanding of the real exposure you have to the market. For example, if the Beta of a stock is 1.5, historically, when the market moves 1 percent, the stock moves 1.5 percent. This is very important to understand, as a portfolio with a heavy concentration of high beta stocks will be much more volatile than the market. At our firm, we always "beta adjust" our portfolio, so we understand exactly how it should act.

B. **Volatility (Standard Deviation):** Many institutional managers prefer to measure the risk of their portfolio by how volatile it is on a daily, monthly, or yearly basis. By measuring how much the portfolio changes on an absolute basis and/or relative to the markets, they are able to compare themselves to each other and the market as a whole on a risk-adjusted basis. It is important to understand that, while you may have an investment that performs quite well, the risk of this asset needs to be taken into account. For example, many investors in housing from 2005 to 2007 did not consider the downside associated with their investments. Volatility can cut both ways, so make sure you understand the risk of your portfolio. Many brokerage firms offer solutions to measure the standard deviation of a portfolio, so check with your particular provider or change to a new one which provides a strong risk management platform.

C. **Value at Risk (VAR):** Similar to standard deviation, value at risk, which was developed by J.P. Morgan in the mid-1990s, takes a holistic approach to measuring the risk of your portfolio. In this case, it looks at the absolute dollar changes of the components of your portfolio and calculates with either a 95 percent or 99 percent probability the absolute loss or gain your portfolio is likely to experience daily.

## Other Portfolio Risk Considerations

### Leverage

Most investors utilize low levels of leverage. However, with proper risk management and portfolio construction, leverage is a tool that can be utilized efficiently. If you have the proper strategy in place, moderate leverage can act as an important tool for additional performance. Utilizing too much leverage can become problematic, as many investors who bought real estate with little money down and little income to support payments came to realize.

### Exposure

Many investors have the ability to both buy stocks and short stocks. If this isn't an option for you, you should focus on the level of cash held in your account. Gross and net exposure are important risk management tools. Exposure is simply how much you are exposed to the market. For example, if you have $1,000 in your account, and have $500 invested, your net exposure is $500 / $1000 = 50%. This means you are 50 percent exposed to the markets, and one could assume you believe that the markets are overvalued, since you are holding a high proportion of your investable assets in cash.

## Hedging

Diversification provides automatic and passive risk management, but many times active management of your portfolio is needed. Over the past few years, many types of alternative securities and strategies have been developed to help an investor gain or reduce exposure to a particular asset class or portfolio; to help him or her hedge a unique problem or create a certain risk profile for a determined period of time. There are generally two types of products used for this purpose:

A.  Derivatives (Options)
B.  Exchange-Traded Funds (ETF)

**Derivatives:** Most investors understand how to utilize options to their advantage. Whether it is buying or selling a call or a put option, the investor gains leveraged exposure for a predetermined period of time. In many cases, it is a smart decision to utilize options in this manner; however, options can play a permanent role in your portfolio management strategy. For example, because many of us suffer from being human, causing us to make or not make rational decisions, options can help "auto-adjust" the portfolio when we are unable to make key decisions.

A.  We make the right decision to buy a stock, and then the stock moves up and we wish we had more. In this case, even though our price target is higher, we hate the idea of paying "up" for a stock we bought at a much lower price. With options, we can own a small position and buy a few call options, thus ensuring that if the stock moves up, our exposure will increase, and since we did not utilize all our capital, should it remain at this price or move lower we can either buy more or exit the position with a smaller loss than had we bought a full position up front.

B.  In the reverse situation, we own a stock that is under pressure, and again, since we are human, it is hard to sell. We are constantly in a state of "hoping" it will go back up so that we may sell it at a higher price. In this situation, had you supplemented a core position with call options, your exposure would shrink as the stock fell, essentially "auto-selling" for you. Another method would be to buy puts on your position as a hedge, should the stock come under pressure, with the same result.

Now imagine this strategy on an entire portfolio. By adding options to your strategy, your entire portfolio can self-adjust as the markets move higher and lower, increasing your exposure to stocks and markets that are working and lowering your exposure should the stocks or market come under pressure. Of course, if this strategy were free everyone would be doing it, but options come at a price, and it is important to understand which methods offer the best value. As in many parts of this book, it is beyond the scope to deeply drill into each particular situation, and the pricing of derivatives themselves can be quite complicated, but one can look at the volatility of an option as a key determinant of its value. Having discussed volatility earlier in this section, we can understand that the more volatile the security we are trying to hedge, the more expensive its option prices are likely to be. Also, when the market is extremely volatile, options will also become more expensive. A common way to grasp how the market is pricing in volatility is to look at the VIX, a measure of the market volatility. Generally, a VIX under 30 is considered consistent with low volatility and lower options prices.

**Exchange-Traded Funds (ETF):** Over the past five years the use of ETFs as a method of risk management and of gaining targeted exposure has exploded. In fact, many investors utilize the inherent diversification in an ETF as their main source of exposure. ETFs by design are composed of many different stocks, and thus provide diversification benefits! In addition, given the rise in their popularity, an investor can find an ETF for almost any type of exposure or hedge. There are literally hundreds of ETFs to choose from, but make sure to take into account three factors when choosing one:

1. **Liquidity:** How large is the market capitalization of one ETF relative to others in the same sector? In general, the larger the better.

2. **Concentration:** ETFs are a collection of securities in a particular market or segment. For example, the XLB is an ETF for the materials sector. However, be cognizant of the size of the portfolio holdings; in the case of XLB, Monsanto (MON) is over 12 percent of the fund. Especially for emerging market funds, such as the EWZ (Brazil ETF), some industries are highly favored (energy, in this case).

3. **Fees:** All ETFs charge fees, some more than others. As a general rule, the larger the ETF, the lower the fees.

The other benefit to utilizing ETFs is their lower volatility, thus making them a great vehicle for derivatives management. If, for example, you own a highly volatile stock and the premium charged to hedge this position is too high, perhaps you can find an ETF that either has this stock as a component or is exposed to the same industry. It is likely the volatility and premium price will be substantially less, yet you will receive similar hedging benefits.

## Stop Loss

Perhaps the easiest but least used risk management tool to understand is the concept of limiting your losses to a specific percentage or number. It is hard to sell your losers and it gets harder the more you lose. I recommend limiting your losses to 10 percent on any position, whether long or short. When the 10 percent benchmark is breached, cut the position in half. This doesn't mean you can't buy that position back, but it does suggest that your due diligence was potentially flawed and you need to revisit your thesis. There is no doubt that with this strategy you can miss terrific buying opportunities, but the savings from implementing this strategy well offset the lost opportunities. There is a reason for the old saying about "throwing good money after bad," and sometimes it really is time to move on to the next opportunity—especially when your stop loss is reached.

## Discipline and Process

The process and discipline for implementing your portfolio strategy should be consistent and defined as well. Certainly, as markets and economic cycles shift, especially during short time periods such as we saw during 2008 and 2009, your priorities might change. But the structure should remain relatively constant over the long term. Factors you should consider and implement include:

A.  Total number of positions to be held.
B.  How big the positions can become.
C.  Composition of the positions (small, medium, large capitalization).
D.  Types of securities utilized (stocks, bonds, options, futures).
E.  Amount of leverage utilized (sometimes called gross exposure).
F.  Risk tolerance, both on an individual and a portfolio basis. Importantly, how do you react when risk levels are breached?
G.  Overall net exposure of your portfolio. This is simply longs minus shorts, or if you are only buying stocks, the formula is long exposure/total assets.

**Figure 8.1 Sample Portfolio Characteristics**

| Portfolio Metrics | Individual Investment |
|---|---|
| Gross Exposure: 100% – 150% | Sizing Based on Score |
| Net Exposure: -20% – 60% | Stop Loss Policy: |
| | Sell ½ Position after 10% loss |
| **Average Exposure: 20% – 50%** | Technical Analysis |
| | Review Charts Weekly |

| 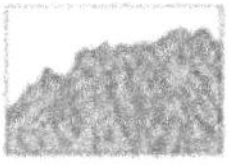 | Initial Sizing | Appreciation Objective | Timing/Holding Period | Max Sizing |
|---|---|---|---|---|
| **Longs** | 1 to 4% | 40 to 100%+ | 3 Months to 1 Year + | 10% |
| **Shorts** | 1 to 2% | 20 to 40% | 3 Months to 6 Months + | 8% |

Any serious investor must consider a well-thought-out philosophy as to how his or her portfolio should look and act. Importantly, if you have defined many characteristics of your portfolio, you are then in a position to measure your success or failures and change if necessary. Similar to individual stock selection, portfolio management and risk management are essential elements to investment success.

## CHAPTER NINE

# Market Strategy

## How to Manage and Understand the Volatile Stock Market and Economy

The final chapter discusses risks that are difficult to determine, yet have a profound impact on our performance: ***market risk***. Even if you have the right stocks at the right time, and have a strong portfolio and risk management, market direction plays a large role in wealth creation.

There was a time, not too long ago, when it was more important to pick the right stocks than it was to time the markets. That is no longer the case, as markets and stocks often move hand in hand. The good news is that over the past five years, many changes have made implementing market strategy both very accessible and inexpensive.

### Market Analysis

Everyone—and I mean everyone—has an opinion about the direction of the global markets. Having said this, the best managers can do well (or lose less) in almost any market, since they deploy many of the portfolio and risk management techniques talked about in chapters 8 and 9.

We will consider three variables in our quest to understand why the market is where it is and what the probable future holds. Importantly, since the market can shift in a new direction based on new information, we need to figure out which variables will create this change and factor it into our strategy:

1. Economic Strategy
2. Fundamental and Technical Strategy
3. Liquidity (Monetary and Fiscal Stimulus) Strategy

## Economic Strategy

Economic performance is ultimately the most important factor in determining the likely course of the markets, but oftentimes the data you see in the present does not accurately reflect what might be happening six to twelve months into the future. Investors are always trying to divine the future. There are three types of indicators used for economic analysis:

1. **Leading Indicators:** These are indicators that tend to point toward the future of the economy. We look to these indicators, such as bond yields, in order to see the road ahead.

2. **Lagging indicators:** These are indicators that lag the economy and tell us more about the past than the future. Unemployment figures are the best example, since by the time people start hiring, the economy and the stock market have already moved up significantly. These metrics are important, however, especially as a confirmation tool for leading indicators.

3. **Coincident Indicators:** As the name implies, these indicators come at the same time as the underlying markets. Personal income is a coincident indicator. When the economy recovers, for example, the employed begin to have more income.

## Best Indicators

**Leading Economic Indicators (LEI):** The most common measurement is called the LEI, and it attempts to forecast the economic future. Composed of eleven specific leading indicators, a move of the LEI in the same direction for three consecutive months reflects the direction of the economy. There exists much controversy with regards to this metric and its validity, since most of the components have already been released, yet it continues to be an important indicator and one that should be utilized in conjunction with others. This indicator is released monthly, generally around the middle of the month. This same metric is also released for many other countries, and I would suggest monitoring it for both Europe and China as well.

**Bond Yields:** Bond yields and, more specifically, the yield curve have a long history with respect to the prediction of recessions. Their inherent predictive powers with respect to economic growth are less acknowledged. Typically, when the yield curve becomes inverted, meaning short-term rates are higher than long-term rates, a recession is on the horizon. Conversely, if long-term rates are higher than short-term rates, economic growth is likely. The government has great control over short-term interest rates, and even if the yield curve looks good, it could be because the government is creating significant liquidity for near-term interest rates, thus creating an artificially steep yield curve. Governments feel the need to stimulate the economy at times to prevent possible depressions; the events of 2008 and 2009 were likely to produce a global depression had liquidity not been substantially increased.

**Industrial Production:** The true engine of economic growth is production. This coincident indicator provides an important view of how the economy is performing in the present. Released around the middle of the month, industrial production measures the raw volume of goods produced by sectors such as factories, mines, utilities, and other businesses. Data that is released at the same time is **Capacity Utilization,** a measure of manufacturing utilization in the economy. Full capacity utilization is generally considered to be in about 82 to 85 percent, and readings above this level portend possible inflation concerns. Readings below 80 percent provide an indication that there is too much slack in the economy. Together with industrial production, these indicators provide investors with real-time information to either confirm or contradict their views on the economy.

**China:** China presents a very unique case for investors today, since for the next five to ten years it is likely the growth engine of the world economy. For this reason, a smart investor will focus on economic indicators from China as well, including industrial production, manufacturing, and the Leading Index, which is similar to the U.S. LEI.

## Economic Cycle

The economy moves in cycles, from recession to an expansion peak and back again, over and over. A critical tool for investors is understanding which sectors outperform and underperform during each point in the cycle.

**Figure 9.1 The Economic Cycle**

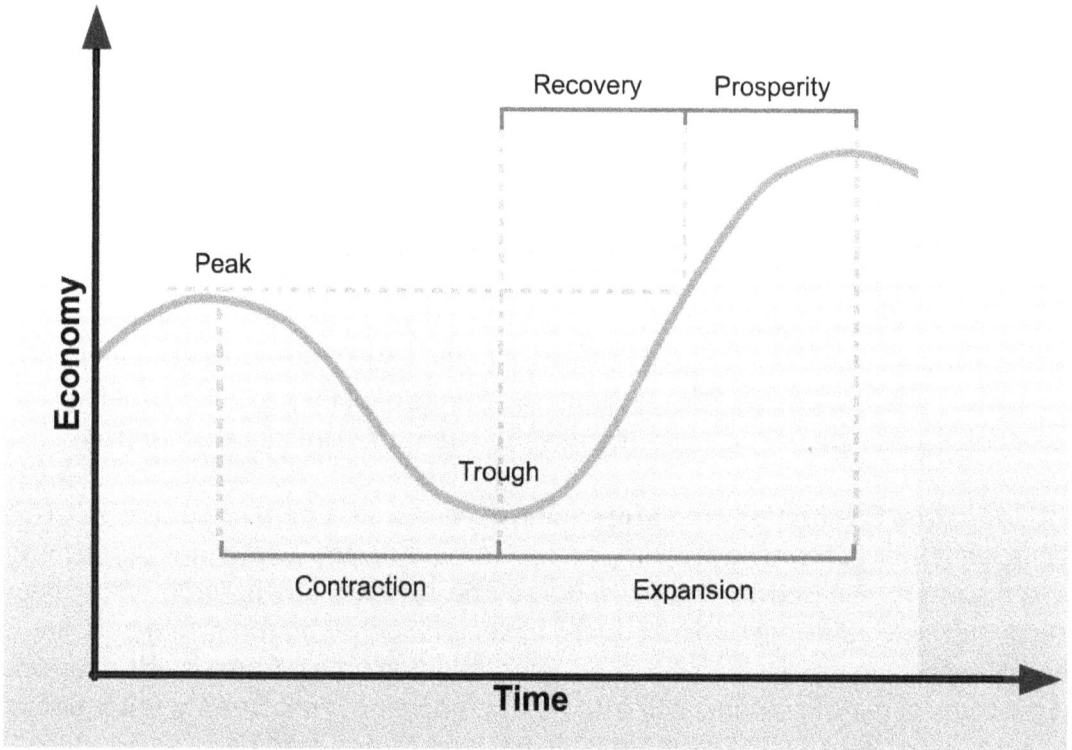

Source: Wikipedia

While a technology stock will certainly perform well during an economic expansion, its best performance (the time it outperforms other sectors) will generally come in the early stages of an economic recovery. This does not mean you sell all your technology stocks as the economy recovers, but recognize that other sectors will start to perform as well.

## Figure 9.2 Sector Performance During Economic Cycles

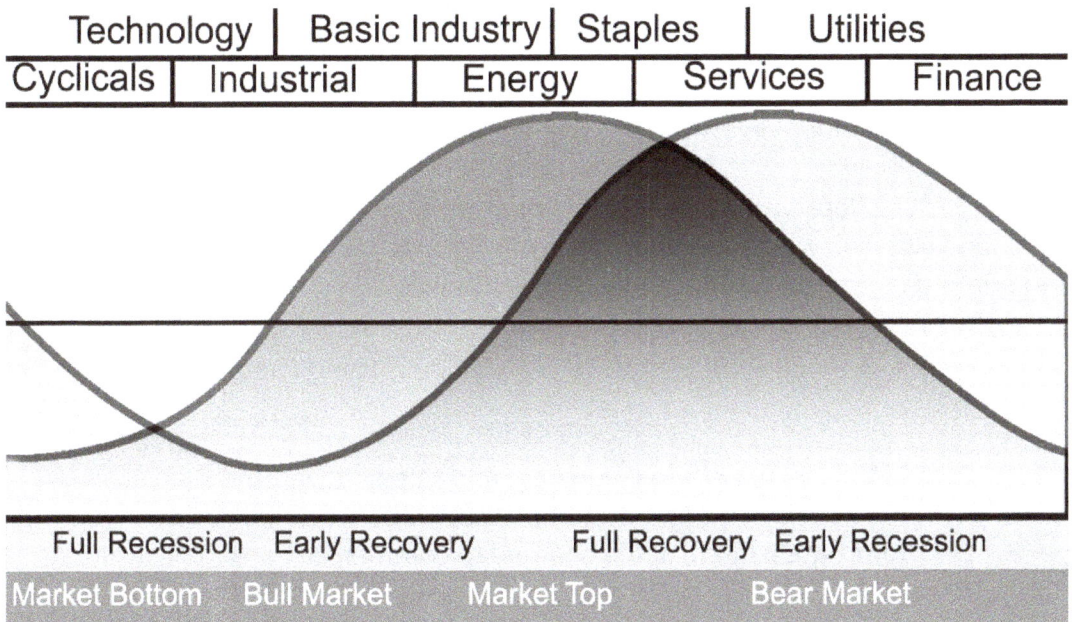

Source: www.stockcharts.com

One strategy that can be deployed during these cycles is the use of ETFs to balance out your exposure. We are fortunate to have so many liquid and inexpensive ETFs at our disposal.

## ETF Exposures to Economic Cycles

| Industry Sector | ETF Security |
|-----------------|--------------|
| Cyclicals | XLY |
| Technology | XLK |
| Industrial | XLI |
| Basic Industry | XLB |
| Energy | XLE |
| Staples | XLP |
| Services | XLV |
| Utilities | XLU |
| Finance | XLF |

## The Federal Reserve: Interest Rates, Currency, and Inflation

This book cannot address the immense and important influences the Federal Reserve has with respect to the economy. Among the many reasons discussed for the financial collapse seen in 2007 to 2009, a Federal Reserve policy of low interest rates and light regulation are among the most prevalent.

The Federal Reserve was created by Congress in 1913, is an independent central bank, and is tasked with controlling the banking system in the United States, including printing currency and effectively setting its value.

There are primarily three methods the Federal Reserve uses to manage the economy:

1. **Open Market Operations:** Purchase and sale of government securities.
2. **Reserve Requirements:** Amount of reserves banks hold relative to deposits.
3. **Discount Rates:** Interest rate charged to commercial banking institutions.

Of these three methods, most managers focus on interest rate policy and discussion through the Fed's Open Market Committee. Interest rates can be utilized to spur the economy during periods of weakness by lowering them, or constrict the economy to keep it from overheating by raising them. As the economy expands, rates will generally rise. When the economy falters, the Federal Reserve will lower interest rates to spur investment. Each month, the Federal Reserve will detail its strategy and any changes it has made to the markets through a Federal Open Market Committee (FOMC) statement. In addition, the Federal Reserve will provide strategic commentary. Generally, this data is well discussed in the media both before it is released (defining expectations) and analyzing its meaning afterward. However, to get a more in-depth review each month, many sites provide a line-by-line comparison to the previous month's statements, allowing investors to draw their own conclusion. One such site is www.marketrewind.blogspot.com. (Search by month with the keywords FOMC Statement.)

## Fundamental and Technical Strategy

We can also measure the markets the same way we measure stocks, both on a fundamental and a technical basis.

Fundamentally, the focus is on:

**P/E Ratio:** Similar to stocks, the major indexes, such as the S&P 500, have valuation metrics associated with them. Monitoring these metrics can give you an idea of where we stand both historically and on a forward basis. For example, in the beginning of 2009, the S&P 500 was trading in the 700 range, or about 10x the previous twelve months earnings. Compared to history, this was very inexpensive. Had you had the courage to believe that we were not facing Armageddon, this metric would have helped give you confidence to start buying.

**Figure 9.3 S&P 500 P/E Valuation**

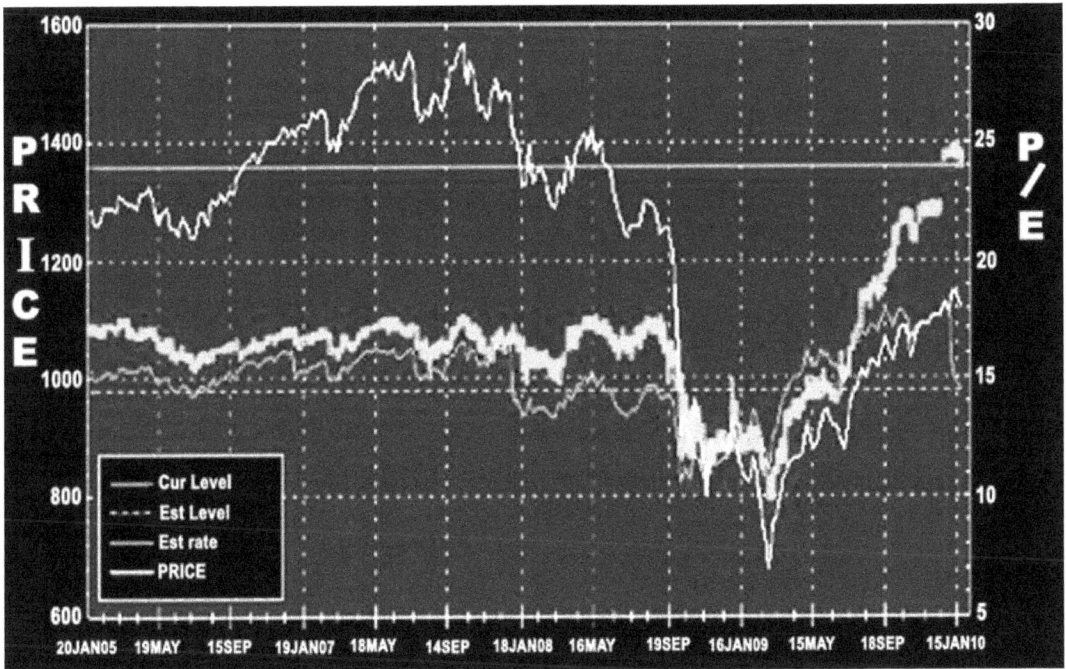

Source: Bloomberg

**Technically**, studying the market is no different than studying individual stock. Traditional methods of understanding and monitoring price movement include moving averages, RSIs, stochastics, and other more advanced technicals such as Point and Figure, Demark Indicators, and Elliot Wave Theory.

## Liquidity

There are times when the market moves in ways that do not reflect the economy, fundamentals, or technicals. This is a very confusing time for many people, both professional and individual. Many times in my career, I have made the mistake of selling

117

or buying too early, getting whipsawed (buying and stocks go down, then selling and they go back up) or having too much cash on the sideline when a major move occurs. Generally, this has to do with periods where abnormally high influence is being directed to the markets, such as the period in 2009 and 2010. With such high levels of stimulus, low interest rates, and government intervention, the market can take on a life of its own as money flows in (and out) of the system.

### Implementation of Market Strategies

Implementing a market strategy can either take the form of a separate action outside of your current portfolio, or it can simply be adjusting your portfolio to your current view.

In the first case, the easiest option can often be the best:

1. Buying or shorting ETFs or futures on an underlying market such as the S&P 500, or
2. Buying or shorting options on an underlying market such as the S&P 500.

In the second case, adjusting your portfolio can be accomplished by:

A. Raising cash by liquidating a portion of your holdings. Take into account that this leads to short-term taxable gains if the holdings are in a positive profit position and are held less than one year.

B. Sell call options—covered call—that are out of the money (OTM) on your long positions. This strategy will give you some protection and will not trigger a taxable event, but if the markets continue to be under pressure, losses will accelerate.

C. Add hedges to your portfolio in the form of buying puts or calls. In effect, you are buying insurance for a portion of your portfolio. Be sure to take into account the cost of this insurance, on an individual basis and as a whole.

Since the direction of the market has a large impact on the profitability of your portfolio, a successful investment strategy *has to* spend time both conducting due diligence and implementing strategies which adhere to both short- and long-term viewpoints.

## ADVANCED KNOWLEDGE

# Technical Analysis Tools
## Additional Methods

### Stochastic Oscillator

Stochastics is a momentum indicator that measures both the support and resistance levels of a stock price or market. This indicator has been used since the 1950s, and in essence looks at the current stock price relative to its historical price range over a period of time and attempts to predict price turning points. The calculation is as follows:

$$\%K = 100 \times \frac{(\text{Close} - \text{Lowest Low for the period})}{\text{Highest High for the period} - \text{Lowest Low for the period}}$$

$$\%D = 3 - \text{period moving average of }\%K$$

There are a few factors to consider with this indicator:

1. If a prevailing price trends is strong, closing prices generally close in the same direction as the trend itself. In a downward trend, the closing price should be near the lows of the trading range, and in an upward trend it should be closing near the top of the range. In these cases, the current prevailing trend is likely to continue.

2. Similar to other indicators, the stochastic oscillator ranges from zero to 100 and signals both overbought and oversold conditions. For example, when the indicator is above 80, possible overbought conditions are present, and vice versa when the indicator is below 20. As you can see from the J.P. Morgan chart below, indicators can remain in an either overbought or oversold position for long time. As with all indicators, utilize them in conjunction with a full analysis and not as a single source.

3. The oscillator contains two lines, %K and %D. The %K is the line that measures the momentum and the %D is simply a moving average of %K generated to smooth out the data and produce more consistent signals.

### Figure 10.1 JPMorgan Chase Chart

Source: www.stockcharts.com

As you can see from the chart above, the indicator does a great job, particularly in calling turning points after a period of weakness.

## Moving Average Convergence Divergence (MACD)

This indicator was developed by Gerald Appel in the 1970s and is meant to measure the difference between a fast and slow exponential moving average. The MACD is generally meant to be a trend indicator (as opposed to the momentum indicators); it is comprised of two lines and sometimes a histogram:

1. The first line, called the MACD, generally in blue or black, is typically the twelve-week exponential moving average (EMA) minus the twenty-six-week EMA.
2. The second line, often in red, is the signal line and represents the nine-week EMA of the MACD.
3. The histogram is simply the difference between the MACD and the signal line.

This typical set of parameters is written as 12, 26, and 9 for the fast EMA, slow EMA, and signal line periods, respectively.

There are a few factors to consider with this indicator:

1. A trading signal is generated when the MACD line (black line) crosses the signal line (red line).
2. A trading signal is generated when crossing zero.

## Figure 10.2 JPMorgan Chase Chart

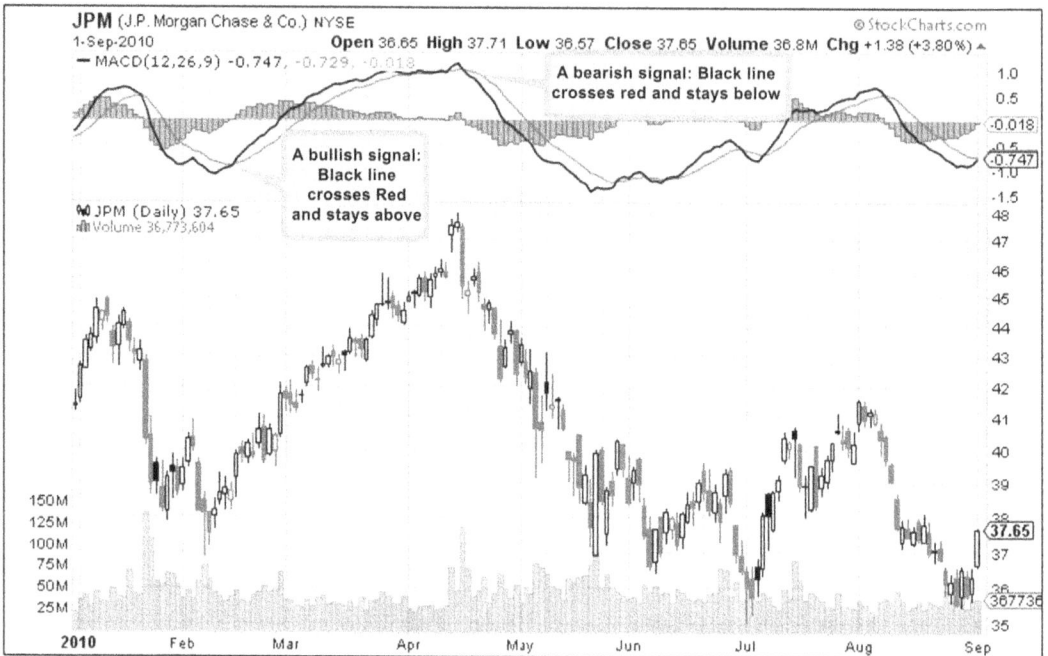

As we can see, in February, the J.P. Morgan MACD line crossed above the signal line at approximately $39, went on to cross over the zero mark, and did not achieve an overbought signal till mid-April, at over $46.

## Advanced Technical Indicators

I have found that Demark Indicators, Point and Figure charts, and Elliot Wave Theory provide very useful information. The costs associated with these products, with the exception of Demark, are trivial compared to the enormous value they provide. The Dorsey (P&F) product helps to identify the medium-term trend of the market. Elliot Wave Theory will help frame the market's cycle and structure dynamics, and the Demark Indicators provide help identifying likely short-, medium-, and long-term levels of price exhaustion (similar information to the RSI).

1. Demark Indicators: Where are we in the trend of the market?
2. P&F Charts: Are investors putting cash to work?
3. Elliot Wave: Where are we in the overall context of market cycles?

## Demark Indicators

Tom Demark developed these indicators over forty years ago to identify likely trend exhaustion opportunities, be they for a single security or an index. He consults on a regular basis with many of the best managers in the business at firms such as Goldman Sachs, J.P. Morgan, and the SAC Group. These tools are considered contrarian by nature and are designed to anticipate price changes rather than react to them.

I consider these tools among the most productive; however, they are only available through subscription and are quite complex to learn. If you are a very active investor with substantial assets or institutional investor, Demark Indicators should be considered seriously. I have been utilizing the Demark Indicators seriously for over five years and wishd I had started sooner.

## Point and Figure Analysis (P&F)

One of the oldest methodologies is Point and Figure (P&F) charting. In fact, Charles Dow, the first editor of the *Wall Street Journal*, was a big fan of this method. In general, P&F charts record the demand and supply relationship within a stock or market. In simpler terms, if there are more buyers than sellers, stocks move up (bullish signals denoted by X's). Conversely, if there are more sellers than buyers, stocks go down (bearish signal denoted by O's). P&F charts this action and is thus a money flow indicator, which can help you figure out who is winning the war, buyers or sellers!

It is beyond the scope of this book to describe this methodology in detail, as it looks much different from traditional charts. Tom Dorsey, who operates a very successful Web portal (www.dorseywright.com), is one of the preeminent experts in the field and provides all the tools necessary at a very reasonable cost, along with a free trial. Similar to the Demark Indicators, I have been utilizing P&F, particularly for market analysis, since 2005, and I wish I had learned it sooner.

**Figure 10.3 JPMorgan Chase Point and Figure Chart**

**J.P. Morgan Chase & Co. (JPM)** NYSE

01-Sep, 16:00 ET, daily, H: 37.708, L: 36.571, C: 37.648, Chg: +1.377

No New P&F Pattern

Traditional, 3 box reversal chart

Bullish Price Obj. (Rev.): 52.0

© StockCharts.com

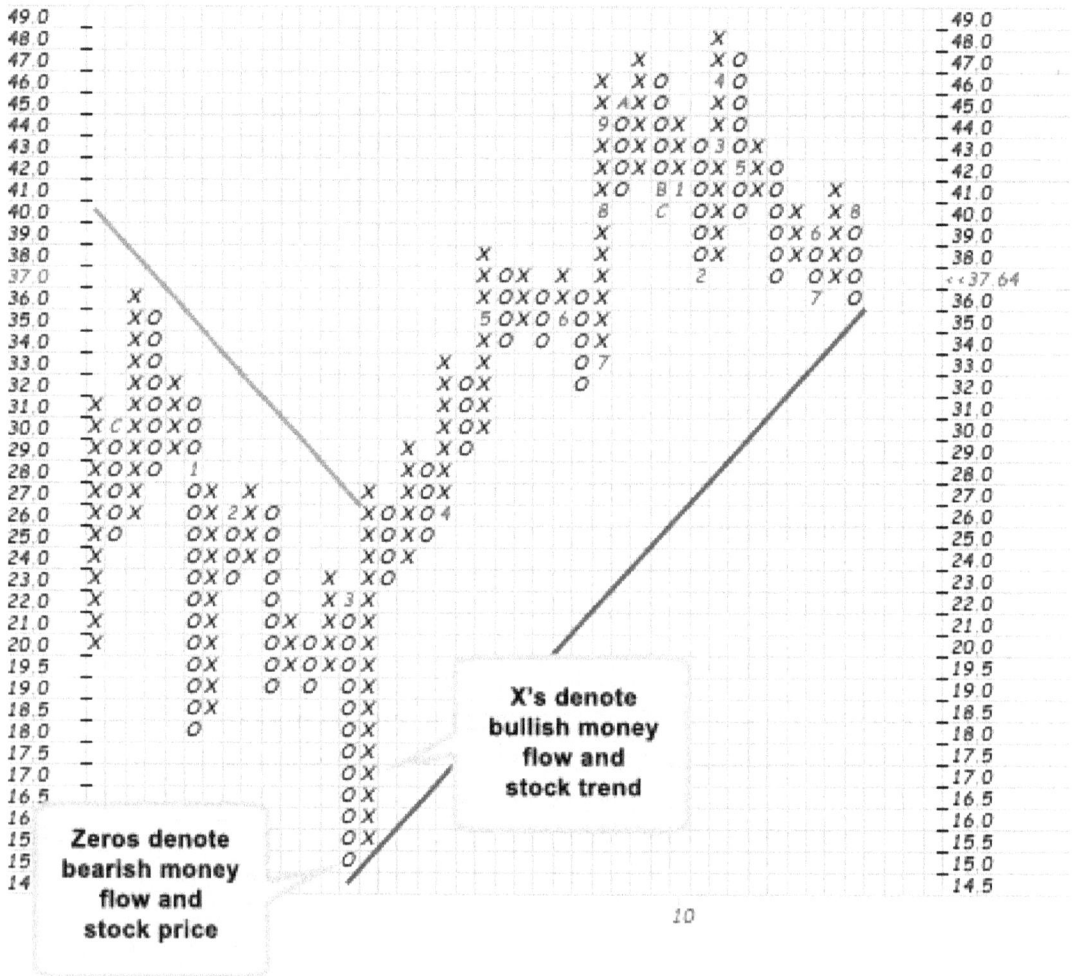

```
49.0                                             X             49.0
48.0                                         X   X O           48.0
47.0                                     X   X O               47.0
46.0                                 X   X O   4 O             46.0
45.0                                 X AX O   X O              45.0
44.0                                 9 OX OX   X O             44.0
43.0                                 X OX OX O 3 OX            43.0
42.0                                 X OX OX OX 5 X O          42.0
41.0                                 X O   B 1 OX OX O   X     41.0
40.0                                 8       C   OX O OX   X 8 40.0
39.0                                 X           OX   OX 6 X O 39.0
38.0               X                 X           OX   OX OX O  38.0
37.0               X OX   X   X               2       O   OX O 37.64
36.0       X       X OX OX OX                             7  O 36.0
35.0       X O     5 OX O 6 OX                                35.0
34.0       X O     X O   O OX                                 34.0
33.0       X O     X   X     O 7                              33.0
32.0       X OX    X OX        O                              32.0
31.0    X  X OX O  X OX                                       31.0
30.0    X C X OX O X OX                                       30.0
29.0    X OX OX O  X   X O                                    29.0
28.0    X OX O  1   X OX                                      28.0
27.0    X OX   OX   X  X   X OX                               27.0
26.0    X OX   OX 2 X O X OX O 4                              26.0
25.0    X O    OX OX O X OX O                                 25.0
24.0    X      OX OX O X OX                                   24.0
23.0    X      OX O  O X   X O                                23.0
22.0    X      OX   O   X 3 X                                 22.0
21.0    X      OX   OX   X OX                                 21.0
20.0    X      OX   OX OX OX                                  20.0
19.5           OX   OX OX OX                                  19.5
19.0           OX   O  O OX                                   19.0
18.5           OX        OX                                   18.5
18.0           O         OX                                   18.0
17.5                      OX                                  17.5
17.0                      OX                                  17.0
16.5                      OX                                  16.5
16                        OX                                  16.0
15                        OX                                  15.5
15                        O                                   15.0
14                                                            14.5
                                 10
```

X's denote bullish money flow and stock trend

Zeros denote bearish money flow and stock price

## Elliot Wave Theory

Ralph Nelson Elliot, an accountant, developed the Elliot Wave Theory in the 1930s. This strategy relies on the precept that market prices unfold in specific patterns, or what Elliot traders call "Waves." Elliot published many books, starting with *The Wave Principle* in 1938.

The theory posits that repetitive waves are formed as investors move from levels of optimism to pessimism and back again, and an investor has an opportunity to profit from the ability to anticipate these waves.

Fortunately, similar to P&F charting, there is a Web site that offers a reasonable subscription rate (www.elliotwave.com). Elliot Wave analysis will help you understand where the overall markets are trading relative to history. This theory will also provide a strong long-term base to your short-term thinking.

**Figure 10.4 Elliot Wave Theory**

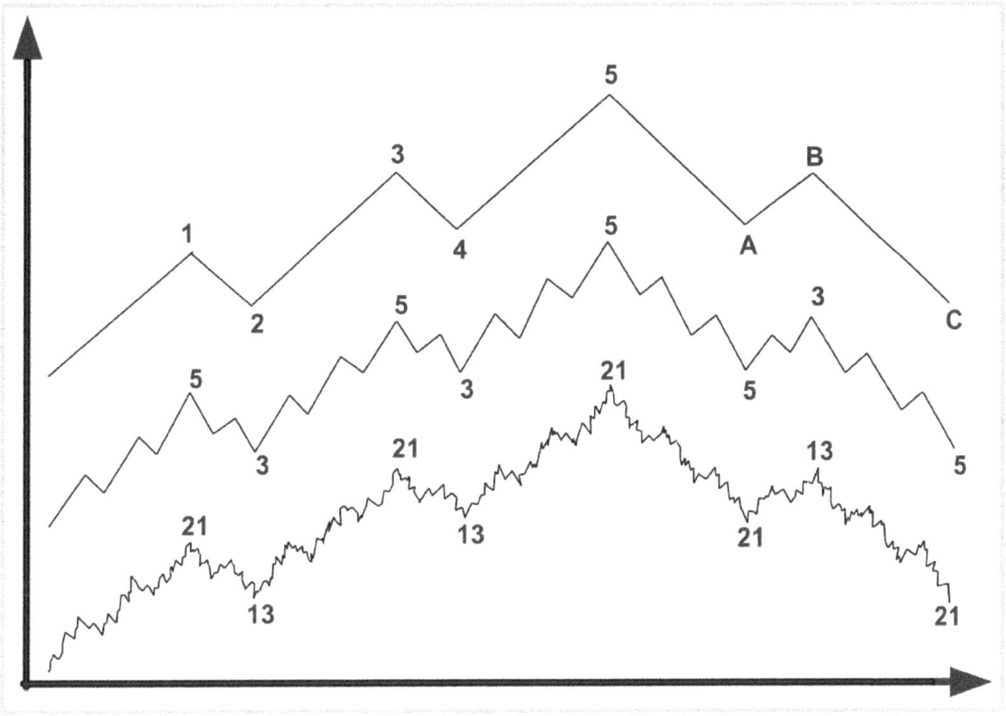

**From R.N Elliott's essay, "The Basis of the Wave Principle," October 1940.**

Source: www.wikipedia.com

# Management Interaction
## Guidelines for Speaking with Management

A partner of mine developed a training tool for use in discussion with company management. Sometimes we have a chance to interact directly with the management teams. Below are the training tools we used for our employees.

### Management Interaction Guidelines

1. Always act as an owner of the stock and lover/believer in the company. Go so far as to use remarks such as, "Your execution capabilities are without peer." As in life, flattery usually *will* get you somewhere.

2. Flatter the company members. Tell them that they are the *best* management team, that you are *so* excited about their products/services and position, that theirs is the greatest company ever. You may not believe it, but you can be sure that *they* do. And if they find you agree with them, they will likely be more forthcoming.

3. Don't try to consult or recommend action. Let them tell you what their strategy is. That doesn't mean to be soft: *always* push them on their financial estimates, such as revenue and margin growth.

4. Push the limits in whichever direction they lead you. Make them "prove you wrong" and "set you straight."

5. Start off focused on products and strategy. It is this big picture, fuzzy stuff that companies usually love to talk about. After that, zero in on the specifics. Focusing initially on a specific topic such as margins does not usually engender openness.

6. Try to make a personal connection with management and help them identify with you. Remember, they need to trust *you* as well. By focusing on the big picture, you become a trusted investor, excited about their opportunities. Once this trust is established, they feel comfortable, opening up a bit about the specifics.

7. Use a long-term perspective as much as possible when posing questions. Ask about short-term perspectives "only to fill in your financial model and as means to prepare hedges." Employees of a company usually think about the long-term, and they appreciate a similar perspective from you. Even if you are in the investment for the short term, act *as if* you're in it for the long term.

8. Stay away from absolute numbers at first. Talk instead in percentages and by comparison. Regulatory changes on Wall Street—in particular Regulation Fair Disclosure—mean that executives cannot (and will not) reveal information to you and you only. If you force them to give you the "Reg FD speech," they're only going to be annoyed.

9. When talking about specific line items on the income statement, feel free to start at an extreme, far outside the realm of established guidance. Let them rein you in and guide you toward reality.

10. If you get the "Reg FD speech" on specifics, respond that you are not looking for guidance or updates, just trying to understand leverage points, realistic growth opportunities, and the like.

11. If you continue to get the "Reg FD speech," tell them that Reg FD refers to full disclosure, not *no* disclosure or privileged disclosure. You can even say that you know your friends at big funds up in Boston are getting more detailed responses from the company.

12. Be *nice*, friendly, and upbeat. It is a conversation, after all, and you will get further if they enjoy talking to you.

13. That said, try not to shoot the breeze too much unless you have a very close relationship. Let them know that if they are cooperative you won't waste their time and will get out of their hair.

14. If they are being uncooperative or stonewalling you, keep circling back to the issues they stonewall you on—don't let them think they can get away with it.

15. Once you've told them what your model looks like and what you're assuming, ask if you're being too aggressive or too conservative. Highlight things going *for* or *against* them as reasons why your views are different from those of Wall Street.

16. At the end of the discussion on the model, review your model "just to let them know how you're thinking about things," and then wait for reactions—silence can be painful, but try to wait.

17. If a company told you one thing, then reported or did another thing, they must be informed that they can't treat you that way. Call *ASAP* after the event, imply you could be fired, that your fund has retirement money in it, or that you are investing your own retirement money. Explain that you felt misled, or that the communication was poor. Beat them down a bit, but don't lose the contact—butter them up a little toward the end. It is likely that next time they will be more forthcoming, and possibly even feel a bit guilty. If a company misleads you repeatedly, move on to another contact or company.

18. Assume existing trends will continue and let them steer you to reality.

19. Use seasonality, market share gains, and strong/new products or lack thereof to push your estimates far lower or higher than the street and see if they resist.

20. Make strong assertions and tempt them to prove you wrong. It's hard for people not to comment when you make things black and white and you're wrong!

21. Ask about conferences: when will you next present? What will the message be?

22. Use technical or specifics to put meat on the bones of the conversation. When you do start talking specifics, it's important that you do have some level of knowledge about the current environment. Oftentimes, you can search the

Internet for recent reports, or, if you are a professional, pull the latest analyst notes.

23. Always assess your contact: How much does this person know? Is this person honest? This can be measured over time and is a great reason to keep a history of your conversations with your contacts.

24. Ask questions and treasure silence. Make them fill in the gap with subconsciously blurted information.

25. Always refer to prior conversations, getting a read if things have changed.

26. Talk about both the bullish and the bearish case with them. You will always get why you should buy the stock. You want to know what they say to those who would tell you to short the stock.

27. Even if you short their stock, compliment them and get them to comment on why the shorts are wrong.

Interacting with management is one of the most challenging aspects of the investment process, but with time, patience, and practice you will find enormous benefits.

## ADVANCED KNOWLEDGE

# Structuring Your Day
## All You Need is a Few Hours

To make the best and most productive use of your day, here are a few suggestions. If you work in another profession, try to incorporate part of this training into your weekly or weekend schedule.

### 7:00 a.m. – 9:30 a.m.: Early Morning Briefing

Review the previous day's news flow. Make sure you understand any implications for your portfolio or prospective investments. Incorporate this knowledge into your daily strategy (investment execution), as well as into the effects on your mid- to long-term strategy. The early morning work is meant as a "briefing" (hence, www.briefing.com), a way to make sure you have the latest data. Later in the day, you will focus in-depth on anything new from the six categories below:

1. Overnight direction of international markets, primarily Europe and Asia.
2. Company-specific financial results, which can influence the trend of the overall markets or your portfolio.
3. Upgrades or downgrades by Wall Street.
4. Economic calendar.
5. Event calendar.
6. Media reports either in print, video, or online about positions in the portfolio.

### 9:30 a.m. – 12:00 noon: Work on Current Holdings

Work on current holdings. Too many people stop working on a stock once it is in their portfolio. Due diligence includes additional discipline work, new data reviews, adjustments to the scoring system, and increased knowledge of a company's products and markets.

### 1:00 p.m. – 4:00 p.m.: New Investments, Themes, and Strategy/Risk Management

Work on new holdings. Due diligence includes work on new ideas, monopolies, and theme development. Score new stocks and review stocks scored previously. Review current portfolio positioning and risk levels, given any new information that may affect your long-term strategy.

### 4:00 p.m. – 6:00 p.m.: Post-Market News Flow

News is continuous, but pay attention to the post-close information. While financial earnings season generally gets started the month after a quarter ends (April, July, October, January), many companies do not follow the traditional fiscal calendar. Also use this time as "flex time," as most of us never get to everything at the appropriate time!

# APPENDIX 1

# Helpful Internet Sites

**The Monopoly Method**
www.monopolymethod.com
www.facebook.com/monopolymethod

**Fundamental Data**
www.sec.gov/rules/final/33-7881.htm
www.retailroadshow.com
www.zintro.com
www.whispernumbers.com
www.wikinvest.com
www.finance.yahoo.com
www.moneycentral.msn.com
www.briefing.com
www.seekingalpha.com
www.wstselfstudy.com

**Commodities Data**
www.futures-research.com
www.greenmarkets.com
www.agweb.com
www.agriculture.com
www.nass.usda.gov/Newsroom/index.asp
www.metalprices.com
www.chinamining.com
www.steelonthenet.com

**Technical Analysis**
www.dorseywright.com
www.elliotwave.com
www.tomdemark.com
www.bigcharts.com
www.stockcharts.com

# About the Author

Greg McCall is the founder of Rock Crest Capital, LLC, an alternative asset management firm based in Norwalk, Connecticut. He has spent the past twenty years working with technology, consumer, and energy companies as a hedge fund manager and venture investor. Prior to founding and managing Rock Crest Capital, a $175-million fund in 2007, Greg was managing director at Westway Capital, a $990-million hedge fund focused on technology markets, as well as companies and industries significantly altered by technological progress. He co-managed a direct investment portfolio of both private and public companies. He has consulted with and/or invested in private companies, including Greenfield Online, SuperWater Solutions, Earth Markets, Yipes!, and Tantivy Communications. Before Westway Capital, Greg was an early partner at Dietche & Field Advisors, a $5-billion investment fund. Acting as an analyst/portfolio manager, he directed investments in the technology sector. During his career, Greg has experienced, firsthand, best practices management from start-up ventures to seasoned public companies, and in addition to serving on various panels, being quoted in multiple publications, and speaking at conferences, he has met and consulted with many senior managers, operating-level employees, and consultants.

He is active civically, focusing his time on helping foster the involvement of parents, leaders, and mentors in the development of at-risk youth in his community. Working with the George Washington Carver Community Center, he built a computer lab and founded a local chapter, Rowayton Connections, which helps raise capital to fund growth and programs at the center.

Greg lives with his wife, Cecilia, and children, Casey and Lexi, in Connecticut.

# Acknowledgments

I would like to thank the many people who helped along the way, as this book is really the culmination of over twenty years of work. From the very beginning, Barry Haimes, founder of Sage Asset Management and a colleague at Dietche & Field, provided much advice during the exciting and challenging years in the investment management industry. I received my start in the industry courtesy of Paul Dietche and Lincoln Field, and I thank them for the opportunity. John Levinson, the founder of Westway Capital, has also been a friend and mentor through the years. When I founded Rock Crest Capital in August 2001, I had no idea how my life would change over the next decade, and I am thankful to all who have contributed to the firm and to the ideas in this book, including Pat Wayland and Mark McCall. There are so many others, including Shellwyn Weston, who taught me the value of hard work and, equally, how to have fun along the way. This book would not have been possible without editorial help from Duff McDonald, contributing editor at *Vanity Fair* and *Fortune* magazines, and author of *Last Man Standing: The Ascent of Jamie Dimon and JPMorgan Chase*. I owe him a great deal of thanks for getting it to the finish line. I also want to thank Pip Coburn, founder of Coburn Ventures and author of *The Change Function: Why Some Technologies Take Off and Others Crash and Burn*, for his candid advice, and for giving me the confidence to finish the book. Lastly, I want to thank my sister, Leslie McCall, associate professor of sociology at Northwestern University and author of *Complex Inequality: Gender, Class, and Race in the New Economy*, for her constant help, support, and encouragement.

Of course, none of this would have been possible without the guidance and love of my beautiful wife, Cecilia, and my children, Casey and Lexi.

# Index